The Ultimate Beginner's Guide to Content Writing

The Simple Guide to Getting to Page One of

Google and Writing Copies that Sell

John Ajayi

DEDICATION

To those who are relentless about creating the future of their dreams.

CONTENTS

ACKNOWLEDGMENTS

I wouldn't know if this book would have been possible if I wasn't opportune to learn from certain experts. Through their courses, videos, and writings, I have become very good at what I do that I teach it.
Thank you Neil Patel, Brian Dean, and Dan Shewan.

Introduction

80% of internet users read your headline, but only 20% read through to the end. An alarming statistic, but the reason is not far-fetched.

Many have failed to understand that you need to grab interest and sustain it. This failure has led to the loss of affiliate marketing revenue for many websites.

Appearing on page one of Google search results is great, converting the traffic is the tough part.

Statistics have shown that readers now skim content. If they don't find what they want in the first few lines, they bounce to other pages.

This book will help you solve that problem.

You will learn, in easy and actionable steps, how to create compelling blog posts, website copies, and highly converting email copies.

Each chapter focuses on a particular aspect and deals with it thoroughly.

You will learn how to craft headlines that grab attention.

Next, you will learn how to write compelling introductions

that will ignite curiosity in the minds of the reader and state the value proposition.

Next, you will learn how to write long-form blog posts. Pillar contents are long-forms and every blog needs one. How do you write 2500 - 4000+ blog posts that readers will read (and not skim)?

You will also learn how to proofread your work. If you don't have a professional editor, what steps should you take to proofread your work?

Writing for the internet is not complete without SEO. How do you write for SEO? You will learn easy ways to write for SEO that will make your articles appear on the first page. I will teach you easy steps I have personally employed to rank as No. 1 on Google for keywords.

In this book, you will also learn how to write emails and website copies. What copywriting techniques convert and what doesn't? What words will paint pictures in the minds of your prospects?

You will also learn the secret hack into getting into Gmail's Primary folder instead of the Promotional folder.

All these are contained in this book and a lot more. The book is easy to read, and there are screenshots and diagrams to illustrate several points.

When you're done with this book, you will start creating online written content like a professional.

Enjoy!

1. THE BIGGEST MISTAKES CONTENT WRITERS MAKE

Writing for the internet is different from any other form of writing. It is a form of writing that places focus on search intent.

Many writers fail to understand that the internet is a marketplace. What results in returns on investment is not necessarily actual sales. Traffic, leads, signups are conversions highly coveted by many websites.

From years of experience as a content writer to serving as a writing coach to several students, I've noticed several mistakes among new content writers, and some 'experienced' ones. Below are thirteen of these mistakes.

Ps. You can have a ha-ha moment when you see a mistake you constantly make.

1. Writing online content like an academic article or a prose narrative

A lot of people who just graduated from college or are looking for life outside the 9-5 take up blogging. This is commendable. However, many of them see writing as an academic piece.

It is not uncommon to see long-form content with no bullet points or subheadings. It is all prose. The only breaks are paragraphs.

Not that these are bad, but if what you are writing is long, use subheadings.

Many health blogs and websites host expert opinions and many of these are boring chunks of very good expert advice.

When you write for the internet, you do it as if the reader is an eleven-year-old.

You break it into smaller points so that the reader can consume the whole piece easily.

According to research published in The Guardian in 2018, people now skim content. They look out for points. They don't read deeply any longer. And that's the audience you're creating content for.

2. Writing in flowery language.

I get a lot of mentorship requests. While listening to some students talk, they will refer to their poetry-writing experience as a writing experience.

Poetry is good, and I love Langston Hughes. However, you cannot apply the same principles in content writing. You should write simply and directly.

The best content writers use simple everyday words. They don't use big vocabularies to confound readers. They apply the KISS rule: Keep It Simple, Stupid.

Since you're not writing Shakespeare, you can keep the flowery language for your literature works. Some readers live for those.

3. Leaving out marketing

Like I mentioned earlier, the internet is a marketplace. As a content writer, you are a marketer. You are marketing your content.

It may sound weird, but that's the truth. A simple search on Google will return millions of results. Your content can hardly be the only solution to the problem.

Your race is to get to the first page of the search engine results for the keyword or focus keyphrase you're targeting. When you get to the first page, your race is to be the number one or get the featured snippet position.

Your marketing tactics involve optimizing for search engines, having an attractive headline, writing a compelling meta description, and having a selling featured image for picture search.

4. Not writing for SEO

This is an offshoot of the just-mentioned mistake. When you write for the internet, you need to apply the rules of SEO. If not, the article will not rank well or even rank at all.

You need to write with the search intent in mind. You want the search engine algorithm to understand what your work is about.

In this internet age, writing well covers writing for SEO. You must be able to fit the keyphrases naturally and strategically.

Writing for SEO can take extra effort and attention, but it is very important. Search engine algorithms are not human, they are robots programmed to target certain things.

Later in this book, we shall cover how to write for search engines.

5. Not solving problems

If you are not out to solve problems, you should work to provide value in another way. People turn to the internet for quick solutions. Google gets 5.6 billion searches in a day. The bulk of these is for answers.

When you write, identify the pain points and provide solutions.

From the headline to the body of the content, you aim to provide answers and you do this in a very simple and straightforward way.

This does not mean you can't write for the love of it. You just need to provide answers to questions.

6. Not having a conversation

When you write, you need to have a conversation. You need to write as if the person you're writing for is before you.

It will be a one-sided conversation when you're writing, but that's why the comment section is for the reply.

Having conversations in your content will make it more engaging. Your readers will feel involved and connected to you. It will break the barrier and keep them reading for longer.

7. Not having a persona

If you're going to be conversational with your content, you must picture someone in mind. You are not writing to yourself. You must have the picture of the perfect reader in mind.

The perfect reader is the persona. This is the person representing all those who will read your work.

Let's say you're writing about pension funds. You cannot write the same way you will write a review for a game console.

You need to understand the pain points of the average reader. What are they going through? What answers do they seek? What are the peculiarities of this group?

You can get this by visiting forums. To get forums, enter into the Google search box "forum" after the keyword or keyphrase. For instance, golf "forums".

8. Not making a connection

If a movie fails to appeal to you in the first few scenes, you'll most likely move to a new one. That may be irrespective of the fact that your favorite actor is the lead.

This is because you don't feel a connection to what you want, or what makes you happy.

From the introduction, you must establish a connection with the reader. This is done by identifying the pain points. You do this by showing that you understand their problems and you have well-researched solutions outlined in subsequent paragraphs.

If you fail to make a connection in the introduction, the

bounce rate will be alarming. Google studies bounce rates. Once people leave your page in less than 5 seconds, your rankings will drop.

9. Doing a shabby research

A well-researched piece will feature statistics and figures. People love it. Thus, Google loves it.

People want to know the percentage of people with certain peculiarities. They want to be able to make decisions based on facts. This is why you need to put figures and statistics in your research.

If you're writing about how profitable social media is, and you can't tell us that about 3.8 billion people use social media, I may not be fully convinced.

Numbers prove your point. They get attention faster than anything. Showing that almost 40% of American adults are obese will call attention. Now, saying that more than one in three American adults are obese will draw more attention.

10. Lumped-up sentences

Your paragraphs should contain 3 - 4 sentences at the most. You should not lump sentences together. Break it down. This will increase the readability, and help your readers find answers easily.

Don't write long sentences. Keep them short and simple. Use punctuation properly. If you have issues with grammar and punctuations, read Strunk and White's 'Element of Style'.

Don't forget that the simplicity of your content must fit the level of understanding of an eleven-year-old.

11. You're not active and direct

You need to use more active sentences. It shows your confidence when you're writing.

Take this example:

After digestion, glucose is transported through the blood. - **Passive**

Glucose travels through the blood after digestion. - **Active**

Using active sentences is good for SEO and makes your work authoritative. By SEO rules, passive sentences must form 10% or less of the entire work. So, you need to have this in mind when you're writing.

12. Shabby Proofreading

After writing for hours or days, it can be tough going over the whole thing. Your mind is so used to the work that you can easily skip mistakes.

This is why giving your work to someone else to proofread is the best way to go. Why do you think publishing and news houses employ editors? To oppress writers? No. It is to ensure that every piece is fitting for publication.

It is not uncommon for editors to ask writers to rewrite a piece more than three times. Authors may spend two years writing a novel and a year editing it.

If you don't find someone to read your work, you can proofread it yourself.

Later in this book, we shall focus on ways to proofread yourself. Proofreading takes a whole chapter.

13. Not writing frequently

The cliche 'practice makes perfect' cannot be any more true when it comes to writing. The more you write, the better you get

Many writers wait for inspiration or muse before they write. Some others wait till they get a writing job. It's funny, but that's the truth for most writers.

Even when you're not writing for a website, you should write for a blog. Make it a practice to write at least twice weekly.

The reason why most writers find it hard to write for SEO is that they don't do it frequently. The difference between a writer who earns about a dollar or two for a word and the person who earns five cents for a word is expertise.

If you can write an article that ranks on the first page and towers on that page, you will earn much.

You need to become proficient.

2. HOW TO WRITE FOR THE INTERNET

You need to hear this again: the internet is a marketplace. The return on investment is different for everyone, but everyone has a goal. That's attention.

On the internet, attention is highly important.

As a new person to content development, you may be stuck on where to start. Why not start from these six questions?

What's the goal?

If you have a piece to write, you should have a goal for it. It may not be a piece for the internet, it can be a speech. It needs to serve a purpose. That purpose is what you need to understand.

Are you solving a problem? Are you analyzing a concept? You could be a leader downplaying tensions with your speech.

No matter what your goal is, you need to keep it at the back of your mind. It will influence the words you will use, your breaks, punctuations, and flow.

If you don't have a goal for writing, find one. Else, you will have a disjointed piece.

What do you know?

You want to write. Great! What do you know about the subject matter?

How deep is your research? Have you taken the time to read about three to four sources on it?

Your work will serve as a resource for people seeking information. Thus, you need to know a lot about it.

Readers are not stupid. They can detect if you don't know much about what you're talking about in a few paragraphs.

These are people who have seen the problem and want to know if you understand their problems specifically. You can't go beating around the bush on this.

In some niches, you can't write if you don't have experience in that niche. For instance, in the blogging niche, you can't fix a problem if you haven't faced it before.

How do you want it to be?

What idea do you have in your mind about the piece you're about to work on?

Do you want it to be an all-encompassing read? You may want it to be a straight-to-the-point piece that solves the problem in a few paragraphs.

What structure do you have in mind? Have you checked your competitors' pages to see how easy it is to read through?

What can you add that isn't there? I particularly love Backlinko.com's layout. It is one of the best I have seen on the internet. It makes for an interesting read.

To have an idea, go through other pages presenting a similar content to your piece. See how they are written, look at the structure, see what you can incorporate, and find what you can improve on.

Who is your target audience?

Who is going to read that piece of yours? Is it the fashionable lady you're recommending a $300 designer purse to? Or a new blogger looking for the best hosting company?

It can also be that age is a factor with your audience. If your audience mostly comprises millennials, you don't want to write as if they are retired or at the brink of retirement.

Understand the pain points of your audience. What fears do

they have? What solutions are they seeking? What do they know?

These questions are very important in understanding who you're writing to. And ultimately, you need the answers to develop your persona.

What are the points, steps, and subheadings?

If you're writing for search engines, you need to break your work down. For instance, a subheading should have about 200 words.

To make it easy for you to write, and easy for your audience to follow, you need to give the content in parts. Each part focuses on a particular aspect.

You should have a major subheading(s) that will take the H2 tag.

Subheadings after the major subheading(s) will take the H3 tags.

By breaking your work down, search engines can easily understand what your content contains. And it makes it easier for parts of your piece to serve as featured snippets.

How simple can you make it?

One of the most popular websites on the internet is Dummies.com. The website gets an average of 11 million visitors monthly. A lot of people visit the website not because they are dummies, but the word - dummies - says something. It says 'simple'.

People want information in a very simple way. If they wanted it difficult, they would have read the paper of one Prof Nerdy Boring of the University of Whatever.

Use simple day-to-day words that are easy to understand. Write in short sentences. Only have a few sentences that are more than 20 words, if you can't help it.

In a paragraph, don't use more than 4 sentences. Use three sentences mostly.

You should also avoid writing in passive sentences. Write more in active sentences. Only 10% of the entire work should feature passive sentences.

Conclusion

Always use authoritative sources during your research. Anybody with good SEO knowledge can write anything on the internet and still rank as number one on Google. You're dealing with a search engine algorithm, not a group of human beings.

If you are writing a technical piece that requires using technical terms, define the technical terms. Use simple words in the definition. Set the standard to be the level of comprehension of an eleven-year-old.

3. SIMPLE STEPS TO WRITING AN AMAZING BLOG POST

Writing a blog post is like having a conversation with a friend. The only thing different is that you've got to follow some rules. These rules are not difficult. You may be surprised that the rules are just like normal rules of communication.

Since you are out to write an amazing blog post, there are a few steps you need to take. These are aside from grabbing your coffee, getting your computer, and getting ready to work.

Plan

The cliché comes to mind here. 'If you fail to plan, you plan to fail.'

This is very true. It may not be absolute as there is a one in one million chances that you may not fail if you fail to plan.

But do you want to take that chance?

Planning is essential as this is where you answer the following questions:

- What do you want to write about?

- How long do you want it to be?

- What goal(s) do you want to achieve?

- Who is your reader persona?

Everything up here is easy to understand until you get to the last one. Who is a 'persona'?

A persona is your model reader. This is the person you have in mind when you're writing. You cannot write to your superior the way you will write to your childhood friend. The same way you won't write to your blog reader the way you write to your lover.

Successful writers write as if they're speaking to the reader persona. This helps to make the writing personal and direct. It is less formal and more engaging.

Research

I'll let you in on a secret. Many writers have little or vague ideas about what they want to write on. Yet, this does not subtract from the quality of their work. They'd still turn in a highly insightful content you would think was written by a professor in that line.

I studied law, but I have written on a lot of aspects ranging from technology to health. And many of these articles got high reviews.

I may not have an idea of the subject, but 'Google is your friend and Bing is your neighbor.' I do my research on them. And while I do this, I take notes.

When you're doing your research, write down technical terms, and find out about them. Most of them turn out to be simple.

Do not discard an authoritative source. Keep the tab open. You would need to return to backlink or cite to the content.

You must fact-check every assertion you make. You don't want to look stupid. For instance, Dan Pena is a motivational speaker who refers to himself as the '$50 Billion Man'. And truly he is rich. He lives in the Guthrie Castle, in Scotland.

However, the only thing he isn't is that he's not a billionaire. His net worth is currently around $450 million.

Yes, he's still rich, but it is easy to assume he is a billionaire.

Lastly, be accurate with figures and statistics.

Outline

This is where you breakdown the structure of what you want to write on.

You curate your topic, acknowledge the space for your introduction, get your subheadings, put down your sub-points, and note the conclusion.

You don't have to follow this structure religiously. Many times, you may have to drop a point or let go of the sub-points. Things like these happen almost every time.

However, having a structure will make your work easier. You can write without thinking about what's next. You have what's next in your outline already.

If you're writing a blog post, writing in listicles or list format is much preferable. It is easier to read. Google loves it. Internet readers also love it.

Optimize

This is where you apply the rules.

You need to be compliant with search engine rules if your

work will appear in search engine results.

Your content should be optimized for a focus keyphrase. This is the intent you are targeting. You want your work to appear when a particular intent is entered into search engines.

The focus keyphrase, also known as a keyword, is what your work revolves around. For instance, if the focus keyphrase of a piece of written content is "heart healthy", the title might be "10 Ways to Keep Your Heart Healthy".

And in the body of the content, the phrase "heart healthy" will appear several times. Though these also have to be strategically done to be recognizable by search engines,

SEO will be treated in more detail later.

Use Multimedia

According to a study by Microsoft, the attention span of an average human being is lower than that of a goldfish. The attention span of an average human being is 8 seconds. A goldfish has an attention span of 9 seconds.

What this means is that you need to grab the attention of visitors. Pictures and videos are a great way to do this.

Infographics are highly effective in grabbing attention and sustaining interest. They pass the information across in an easy-to-understand way. Many websites create infographics alongside their posts. They also serve as valuable content for Pinterest users.

You can also create videos for your post. It can be a simple video with a music background to slides or one with human presence. Most people would rather see a video if one is available.

However, you can sustain interest in your written content with pictures. Pictures help break up your text. This gives it white space and increases readability.

Screenshots and amateur pictures work better than stock photos. You may be surprised to find several other websites using the same stock photos as you. This can negatively affect your ranking.

Give more at the beginning

This is called "the inverted pyramid" or the "cone principle of information". This simply means that you should get to the point at the beginning of your content.

Getting to the point means stating the goal of the content in the first paragraph. If you're going to show, in steps, how to fix a bike, say it early.

Doing this tells your reader the point you're trying to achieve.

Proofread

Find an editor. However, if you can't, take a short break when you're done writing. Return to it and read it aloud. Do it about three times. You must read slowly line by line.

Conclusion

Just like a conversation, but with an easily distracted listener, developing a blog post requires grabbing attention and sustaining it.

You need to break your work down to make it scannable. Use bullet points and subheadings to improve readability.

4. WRITING HEADLINES

AN OFFER THEY COULD REFUSE

"The Godfather" would never be made today because it's not a Marvel film, its director says

May 1, 2017

By **Ashley Rodriguez**
Reporter

Headlines lead the way to your content. They determine to a great extent if the reader will click on your post in the search engine result.

Three items appear in a search engine result. In this instance, we shall use Google.

www.krusecontrolinc.com › rule-of-7-how-social-medi... ▾

Rule of 7: How Social Media Crushes Old School Marketing ...

Mar 29, 2018 - The Marketing **Rule of 7** states that a prospect needs to "hear" the advertiser's message at least 7 times before they'll take action to buy that ...

www.thebalancesmb.com › ... › Sales & Marketing ▾

Using the Rule of 7 to Radically Grow Your Business

The Rule of 7 is a determination of the average number of impressions a brand must make on a member of their target market before making a sale. Below are ...

The text in blue is the title. Before anyone reads the meta description, the title comes first. If an average user cannot get the point in the 10 words that will appear, it won't attract any click.

The case is the same for native advertising. The only difference here is the picture you use.

Your headlines also matter in social media posts.

You want clicks and shares, but if your headline doesn't draw attention, you may not get any of these. Check out this Hubspot tweet:

HubSpot ✓ @HubSpot · May 13

"A question that every creator staring at a blank canvas right now should be asking: 'How can we help?'" – @meghkeaney

You may know what content shouldn't be published right now – but what content should be? Read more from our VP of Marketing:

A Content Marketing Playbook for Times of Crisis
In uncertain times, helpful content can bring companies and consumers closer together. Learn how to build a content marketing strategy to bes...
🔗 blog.hubspot.com

The headline of the post shows in the tweet. It is direct, concise, and specific.

The Thing About Headlines

*"On the average, five times as many people read the headline as read the body copy. **When you have written your headline, you have spent eighty cents out of your dollar**."* (Emphasis mine)

That's David Ogilvy on headlines. David Ogilvy is the father of modern advertising. His work in advertising was largely done before the internet, yet the principles are ever relevant when it comes to creating copies.

The headline is 80% of your work. According to Copyblogger, 80% of people will read the headline, but only 20% will read through to the end.

This is why a lot must go into your headline.

Creating Effective Headlines

Note: there is no one size fits all solution to creating headlines. Written content differs, but it needs to meet certain standards to be effective.

We're going to be practical here. We shall look at examples of headlines from Upworthy. Articles from Upworthy are some of the most-shared on the internet. They don't follow the traditional rules, yet they get more shares than most breaking news.

Take this headline as an example:

LET'S DO MORE TOGETHER

10 practical and meaningful ways you can take part in this historic moment

By Harmony Hobbs 06.17.20

This headline uses certain words to build interest. It creates a curiosity in the mind of the reader to see which actionable step can be taken.

First. Note the use of numbers. By using numbers, the reader feels like there is a chance for me to see what I can do from my end. Out of ten, one must apply to me.

Second. The use of adjectives also stands out. "Practical", "meaningful", and "historic" add more flavor to the headline. There are other articles on the internet on how to take part in the Black Lives Matter Movement, yet this stands out.

Anyone could have written something like:

"10 Ways to take part in the Black Lives Matter Movement."

And there are articles like this on the internet.

Third. The headline uses personalization. By using the personal pronoun "you", it becomes direct. It speaks to the reader and establishes a connection. It is no longer about ways to participate, but about ways, the reader, in particular, can participate.

Fourth. It tells the point of the article. The reader goes on to read the article knowing what to expect. The article provides actionable ways to participate and this is very clear without having to read the article.

Look at this new example:

POPULAR

Seattle man served with $1.1 million medical bill after 62-day COVID-19 hospitalization

By Tod Perry 06.16.20

This headline brings several things to mind. From asking if the bill was a mistake to thinking if the man was overcharged. Your mind goes to the insurance policy of the man and wonders if the insurer will cover the cost.

With these questions roaming your mind, you want to spare a minute to scan the story. Mission accomplished!

What makes this headline stand out?

First. It tells the whole story. Without reading it, you know what happens and you're likely to share almost immediately.

Second. It uses figures. Numbers attract. $1.1 million is not a small number.

Third. It makes the character a relatable one. Even though the bill seems outrageous, there is a possibility that the patient is a billionaire who wouldn't care about the cost. However, our mind doesn't go there.

Fourth. It draws an emotional response. This man just survived a deadly disease, why give him a heart attack?

The Rules of Writing Headlines

1. Length matters, but not every time

When it comes to flouting rules such as length, Upworthy does it best. However, Upworthy does not rely on search engines for traffic. Their articles get millions of shares and many just love the tone of their content.

But not everyone has that social strength and dedicated readership. If you rely on search engines for the bulk of your traffic, you may need to follow the length rule.

The length of your headline should be 62 characters or 6 - 7 words. This is for it to completely show in search engine results.

Look at this search engine result:

bleacherreport.com › articles › 2794156-nfl-colin-kaep... ▾
NFL: Colin Kaepernick Has Raised Attention, Awareness on ...
The **NFL** issued a statement Tuesday praising former San Francisco 49ers quarterback **Colin Kaepernick** for helping raise awareness of social justice **issues** ...

The headline doesn't give me enough. It has been cut for being too long. The meta description is also long. I don't get the whole story from it. This means that I'm most likely to click on another website.

Now, look at similar results on the same page:

theundefeated.com › features › colin-kaepernick-protes... ▾

Colin Kaepernick protests anthem over treatment of minorities

San Francisco 49ers quarterback **Colin Kaepernick** says he refused to stand during the ...
Kaepernick told **NFL** Media that he did not tell the team he was planning to ... He has been
outspoken on his Twitter account on civil rights **issues** and in ...

theundefeated.com › features › say-goodbye-to-colin-k... ▾

Say goodbye to Colin Kaepernick as an NFL player

NEW YORK — **Colin Kaepernick** has as much chance of playing quarterback ... that need to
happen so, ultimately, we can address this **issue** and create change.

theundefeated.com › features › the-nfl-and-colin-kaepe... ▾

The NFL and Colin Kaepernick are done with each other

The **NFL** is officially done with **Colin Kaepernick**, commissioner Roger Goodell ... On the
former, Kaepernick provided the **wrong** answer by pushing back against ...

The three are from the same website and they are crafted in a way to make you click on them. What stands them out?

First. They summarize the story.

Second. They contain certain words "protests", "say goodbye", and "done". These words carry meanings that draw a reaction.

2. Use Adjectives

When it comes to headlines, adjectives are like spices. They evoke emotional responses and make it interesting to read.

When you write "the best way to...", it calls attention. The word "best" implies that there is none better than what you're offering. Other words like "unbelievably", "incredible", "awesome", "easy", and many others pass messages to the reader.

Look at this Upworthy headline:

POPULAR

The White House made a propaganda video about the protests that might as well be from another planet

By Annie Reneau   06.03.20

Look at the use of an adjectival clause as the last part of the headline. The clause "that might as well be from another planet" tells more about the "propaganda video" and makes you more curious about knowing the content of the video.

Power Words

Power words evoke emotions and curiosity. These are words that are strategically added to ads and sales pitches to boost conversions.

Power words are not exclusively used in sales pitches. They are used in headlines, subheadings, buttons, landing pages, email subject lines, and in many other instances. In this chapter, we're focusing on headlines. Check out the following example from Cosmopolitan

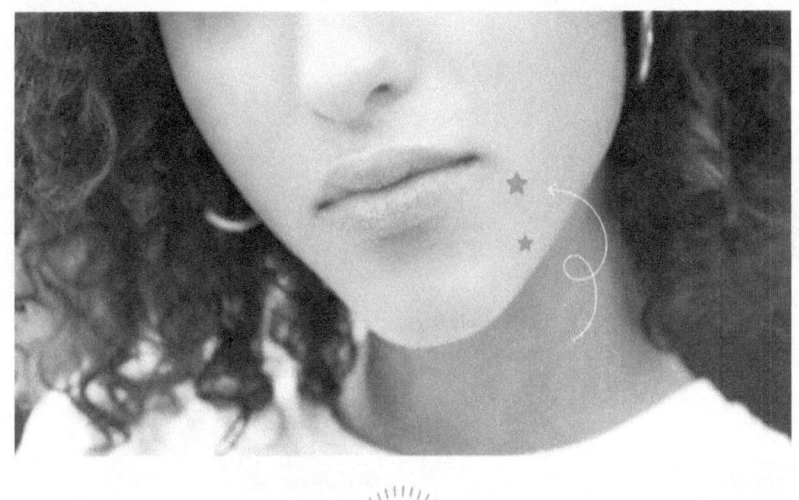

These 10 Face Serums Are Truly Magical for Your Breakouts

Note the use of the phrase " Truly Magical"; it evokes curiosity especially in the mind of someone with the condition. Imagine replacing the phrase with the word "good", will the headline still evoke curiosity?

"These 10 Face Serums Are Good for Your Breakouts"

Still passes the same meaning, but draws lesser attention.

Study these examples to see how Power Words are employed to grab attention:

Look, These Are Summer 2020's Very Best TV Shows

by LEAH MARILLA THOMAS AND LAURA HANRAHAN

The 'Athlete A' Doc Will Stop You in Your Tracks

by EMMA BATY

The Very Best Wedding Reality TV Shows

by HANNAH CHAMBERS AND MEHERA BONNER

20 Psychological Thrillers That'll Freak You Out

by MEHERA BONNER

Notice the use of the word "best" in two of the headlines. Also, note the use of statements that evoke emotions.

"Will Stop You in Your Tracks" and "That'll Freak You Out" are statements that make you want to click on the headlines.

Using Power Words in Headlines

Power words are mostly adjectives in that they tell more about the subject in the statement. You can use more than one power word in a headline. Let's look at this example again:

LET'S DO MORE TOGETHER

10 practical and meaningful ways you can take part in this historic moment

by Harmony Hobbs

06.17.20

The words "practical", "meaningful", and "historic" are power words and they work together to amplify the message in the headline.

Note: a list of 100 power words will be provided at the end of this chapter.

Other Rules of Writing Headlines

- **Use Exact Year**

Apart from the fact that the Google Search algorithm likes recent web pages, more people click on headlines promising current information. For instance:

The Complete Guide to Investing in Bitcoin

The Complete Guide to Investing in Bitcoin in 2020

Market information changes fast and what worked last year may be obsolete now. Reading a guide with current information promises to be more helpful than one that could have been written 3 years ago.

Look at the practical outplay of the example:

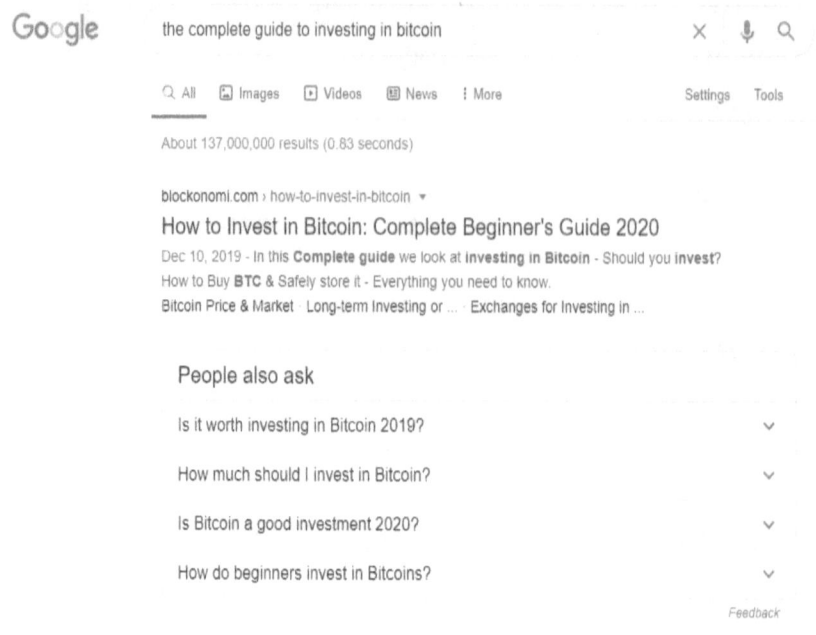

A major factor in the number one position of this page is the year. Look at the "People also ask" section, two questions have specific years in them. Look at the next three results in that page:

www.investopedia.com › Cryptocurrency › Bitcoin ▾
How to Invest in Bitcoin - Investopedia
Mar 16, 2020 - 3 This should not concern most **investors** because **Bitcoin** is legal in the U.S.
and most other developed countries. Step One: Get a **Bitcoin** Wallet. The first thing that you'll
need to get started is a wallet to store **bitcoin**. Step Two: Connect a Bank Account. Step Three:
Join a **Bitcoin** Exchange. Step Four: Place Your ...
Bitcoin How to Buy Bitcoin ... · Bitcoin The Strange New ... · Coinbase · Satoshi

blockgeeks.com › guides › how-to-invest-in-cryptocurr... ▾
How To Invest in Cryptocurrencies: The Ultimate Beginners ...
How To **Invest** in Cryptocurrencies **Beginners Guide**. If you want to buy **cryptocurrency**
quickly and easily with your credit card check out the Kraken Exchange!
Cryptocurrency Wallet Guide · CE101: Introduction To ... · Whitepaper · OmiseGO

hackernoon.com › the-beginners-guide-to-investing-in-... ▾
The Beginners Guide to Investing in Bitcoin & Cryptocurrency ...
To start **investing in Bitcoin** and other cryptocurrencies you first need to sign up to an
exchange which will allow you to buy **cryptocurrency** with cash. An exchange is basically an
online platform that enables anyone to buy and sell **Bitcoin** as well as any other
cryptocurrency that they have listed.

Notice that the second result is more recent than the first, but any people wouldn't notice that. The title draws the most attention. According to Search Engine Watch, the number one position gets 33% of search traffic on Google.

This means that the number one position gets at least one click in every three searches for the keyword it ranks for.

- **Use Numbers - They Attract the Mind**

Numbers are "brain candy". It couldn't have been better expressed by Mike Hammers in a guest post on Write Direction.

As much as people love to get information on the internet, they want it fast and clear. They don't want to read a long essay before they get what they want.

This is why listicles sell. List articles give the promise that the reader is going to get something specific.

Lists also make reading easier. The article is structured and the points are easy to get. Readers can speed-read or skim the content to get what they are looking for.

For the writer, having a well-structured article like a listicle helps to keep the writer on the subject matter. It is easy to veer away from the subject matter when the article has no formalized structure.

Check out this article by Brian Dean on Backlinko:

The headline pulled a lot of search engine traffic that it got almost 15,000 social media shares. As much as the article is highly helpful, the potential reader will have to first discover it via search engines.

Note:

❖ Odd numbers attract more as they seem more

authentic than even numbers. Numbers like 5, 7, 9, 11, 13, 15, 17, 19, 21 send messages to the brain.

❖ When it comes to steps, don't go more than 9. People need something they can easily follow through. Copywriters use 3 and 5 mostly.

- **Provide a Rationale**

A rationale is an underlying reason why something should be done. Providing a rationale increases the chance of boosting your traffic.

Use words like tips, reasons, lessons, tricks, ideas, ways, principles, facts, secrets, and strategies. Look at this headline from Inc.

Apart from using power words like "most" and "powerful", numbers to promise organization and specificity, the use of the word "lessons" gives me a reason to read the article.

- **Be Specific**

Be specific in writing your headline. If you're going to demonstrate how to solve a problem in 7 ways, mention it. If 7 in 10 experts recommend a product or tool, mention it specifically. Instead of saying "most" or "the majority" provide the facts.

Also, focus on a specific point in your headline. If your article is about solving a particular problem, place laser-focus on it. Don't add fluffs or unnecessary elements.

- **Uniqueness**

You don't want to have the same headline as someone else. Chances are the person's website may have a higher domain authority and will rank higher. Spotting the same headline will reduce the interest your headline may have stirred.

When you want to know if your proposed headline has been used by someone else, write it into the Google Search bar and surround it with quotations.

Look at these examples:

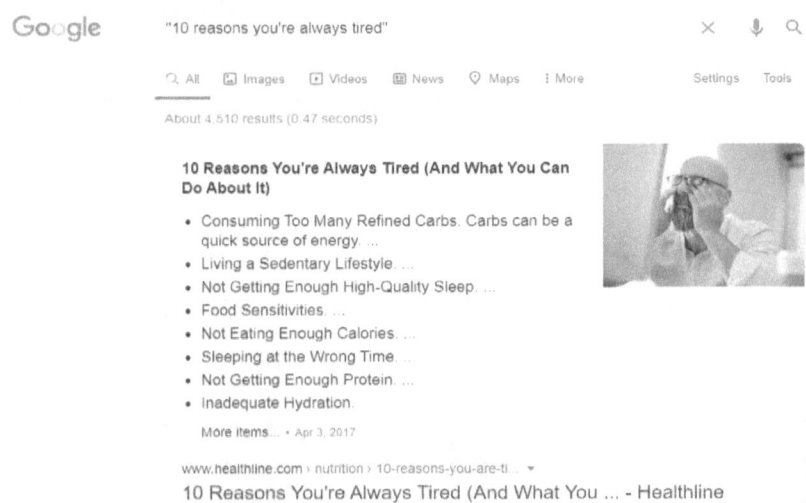

Clearly, someone else has thought of this headline and has used it. It wouldn't make sense if I use the same headline again.

Look at this:

Google tells me that no one has used "10 reasons you're

always jumpy". This means I can use the headline if I am writing something along that line.

Using Headline Analyzers

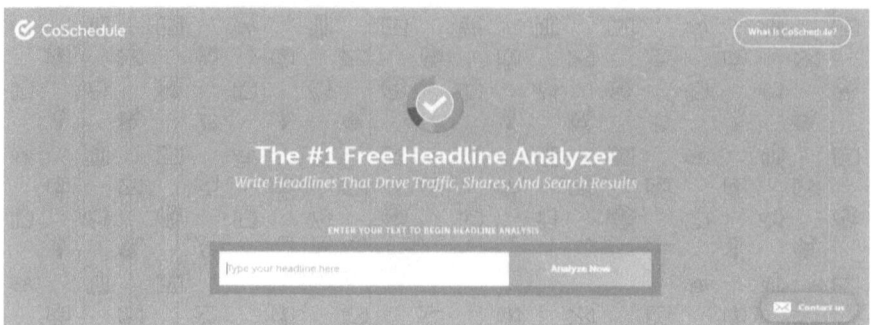

If you're worried that your headline may not grab enough attention, you can run it through a headline analyzer.

Headline analyzers check the strength of emotional appeal in your headline.

They look at the adjectives and the power words you're using to determine how strong and appealing your headline is.

Headline analyzers also consider length, specificity, and structure.

The two most popular headline analyzers are:

- ➢ Coschedule Headline Analyzer
- ➢ The Advanced Marketing Institute Emotional Headline Analyzer

Both tools are free.

However, the thing about headline analyzers is that they're not humans. You can only have an idea of how people will react to it, you're not certain.

It is best to run your headlines through team members. You can also split-test by running $5 Facebook ads to see which one draws more engagement.

- **When You're Stuck**

It is not unusual to be stuck when creating headlines that is why there are several tools to help you.

1. Use Portent's Content Idea Generator.

This free online tool can create headlines based on your keyword. It is meant to be an idea generator if you're stuck on what to write on.

Let's say your keyword is 'car' and you're stuck on the idea for the content. If you run the keyword in the tool, you get up to 20 unique ideas.

Check these out:

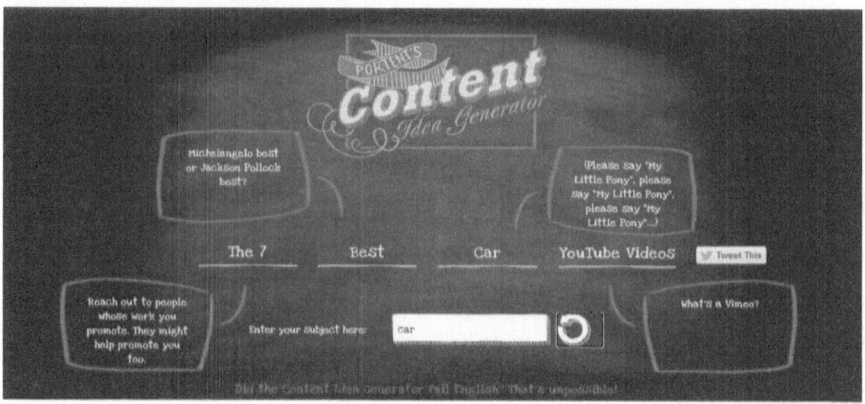

This is an idea for a piece for an article on cars. Check out the others:

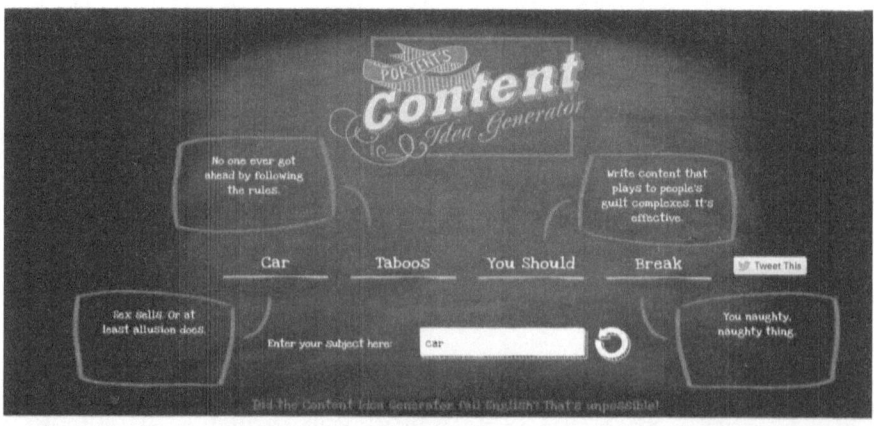

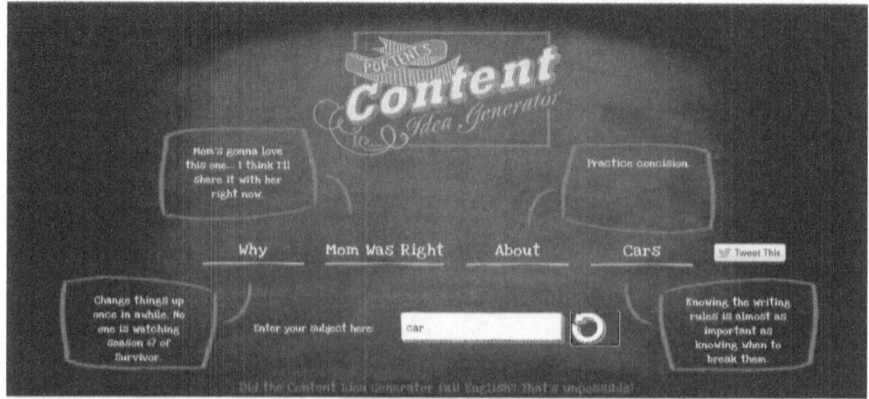

2. Use headline formulas

These are like templates for headlines. All you need to do is input certain details and you will have a complete headline.

Here are 19 headline formulas with examples:

TYPE	FORMULA	EXAMPLE
The How-To Headline	How to (achieve a desired objective)	How to Become a Renowned Writer in 6 Months
The Large List Headline	(large number) Ways or Ideas to (achieve a goal)	77 Ways to Make Money on the Internet
The Ultimate Guide Headline	The Ultimate Guide to (achieve a goal)	The Ultimate Guide to Self-Publishing
The Proven Methods Headline	(number) Proven Methods to (achieve a goal)	21 Proven Methods to Get Rid of Acne
The Mistake Headline	(number) Mistakes that People Make When (common action)	10 Mistakes that People Make When They Fall in Love

The Secrets Headline	(number) Secrets to (achieve a goal)	10 Secrets to Make Anyone Fall in Love with You
The Lessons Learned Headline	(number) Lessons I Learned From/ When (experience)	10 Lessons I Learnt From Reading Elon Musk's Biography 10 Lessons I Learnt When I was 18
The Social Proof Headline	The (object) Over (Social proof) Used to (achieve a goal)	The Tool Over 2 Million Marketers Use to Generate Quality Leads
The See-What-Happened Headline	(person) Did (unusual action) For (Timeframe). Here's What Happened	I Stopped Running for Six Months. Here's What Happened.
The How/ Result Headline	How (a seemingly inconsequential action) (an undesirable outcome)	How Watching TV Damages Your Brain
The How-To Without Headline	How to (desired outcome) Without (unpleasant action)	How to Get Thousands of Quality Leads on Facebook Without Running Ads
The Silver Platter Headline	(number or how to) Simple/ Easy Ways to (desired outcome)	10 Easy Ways to Make an Extra $100 a Day
The Hacks Headline	(number) Hacks to (achieve a desired outcome)	50 Hacks to Make Your Life Easier
Step to Results Headline	(number) Steps to (achieve a goal)	5 Steps to Making a Budget

The Reasons Headline	(number) Reasons You're (outcome)	10 Reasons You're Stuck
The Solutions Headline	Why (problem) And (What to do about it)	Why You're Always Tired and Ways to Boost Your Energy Levels
The Expert Roundup Headline	(number) Experts Share Their (topic)	17 Music Producers Share Their Views on Mumble Rap
The Front-Loaded Keyword Headline	(Keyword): How to (long-tail keyword)	Copywriting in 2020: How to Write Content That Will Rank on Google
The Get Rid Off Headline	Get Rid of (problem) Once and For All	Get Rid of Acne Once and For All

List of 100 Power Words

Trust Words	Greed Words	Captivating Words	Sloth Words
Approved	Affordable	Alluring	All-inclusive
Authentic	Bargain	Amazing	Basic

Authoritative	Barrage	Astonishing	Building blocks
Authority	Bonus	Astounding	Cheatsheet
Backed	Budget	Awesome	Child's play
Because	Cheap	Badass	Clear
Best	Convert	Bomb	Complete
Best selling	Double	Brilliant	Comprehensive
Bonafide	Drive	Catapult	Copy
Cancel anytime	Forever	Charming	Downloadable
Case study	Free	Defying	Easy
Certified	Immediately	Delicious	Economical
Dependable	Increase	Delightful	Efficient
Don't worry	Instantly	Dreamy	Effortless
Endorsed	Money	Epic	Elementary
Expert	Never	Explosive	Fail-proof
Fully refundable	Now	Exquisite	Fill in the blanks
Genuine	Off-limits	Greatness	Formula
Guaranteed	Overnight	Heavenly	Free
Protected	Profit	Incredible	Freebie
Proven	Promote	Jaw-dropping	Gift
Recession-proof	Sale	Kickass	Guide
Recognized	Today	Legendary	How-to
Scientifically-Proven	Triple	Mesmerizing	In less than

Studies show	Unlimited	Mouth-watering	In record time

5. WRITING COMPELLING FIRST STATEMENTS

Imagine going on the first date with someone you're very interested in. This is a date you have been dreaming about all week, and you almost had trouble sleeping the night before the date. What impression would you want to give knowing that first impressions matter a lot?

That's the case with writing introductions. You want to support your attractive headline with a compelling first statement.

If your first statement lacks clarity or fails to compel, all the work you have put into your headline and the body might become useless. Just like first impressions, if you make a terrible one, you may not get the second chance to prove that you're a good person.

An attractive headline is important, but it needs the sturdy support of a compelling first statement or introduction.

(CNN) — Iran has issued an arrest warrant for US President Donald Trump over the drone strike that killed a top Iranian general in January, the semi-official Fars news agency reported Monday.

Trump is one of 36 people Iran has issued arrest warrants for in relation to the death of Qasem Soleimani, commander of the Islamic Revolution Guard Corps (IRGC), according to Fars, but the Tehran attorney general Ali Alqasi Mehr said Trump was at the top of the list.

Mehr claimed Trump would be prosecuted as soon as he stands down presidency after his term ends, Fars reported.

Ways to Create a Compelling Introduction

- Create a Powerful Lede:

A lede is used mostly in journalism to start a news item. It is also known as a lead statement or the introduction.

It grabs the attention of the reader by giving a preview or summary of the story. It is catchy, short, and it heightens interest. Though there are several ways to write a lede, it's sole purpose is to grab attention.

Check out this CNN report of the issuance of an arrest warrant for President Donald Trump by Iranian authorities.

Pay attention to how the first statement summarized the whole story. The introduction makes you want to know more.

Yeah, you may not be a journalist, but this method is also

applicable to creating blog posts. Check out this example:

Career Advice, Watercooler

How Taking a Sabbatical Can Boost Your Career

November 26, 2018 | Posted by Emily Moore

After spending one too many late nights at the office, who among us hasn't fantasized from time to time about leaving all of our responsibilities behind and heading to some far-off location — perhaps the white-sand beaches of Mexico, the rugged mountains of Switzerland or the stunning traditional architecture of Japan. But inevitably, reality sets in: You've got work to do, chores to finish and a steady drumbeat of bills, loans and expenses to pay.

This is from a blog post on GlassDoor. Even though this introduction does not give you a summary of the article, it grabs attention by establishing a connection with the reader.

People who read the GlassDoor blog are professionals, recruiters, or job seekers. This is a story they can relate to.

By standard, creating a lede involves answering the 5 'W' questions: who, when, where, how, what, and why. This is however not absolute.

In journalism, the 5 'W' questions work this way:

What happened? Who is the feature story about? When it occurred? Where did it transpire? How did

it happen?

In creating a blog post about the popular use of smartphones among pre-teens, you can have something like:

"My 9-year-old niece Ashley got her first smartphone in January. So, she can finally take goofy pictures of herself and ask Google the almost uncountable questions she asks daily.

However, one thing I have realized is that she spends a lot of time with the device, and I get worried that the age-restriction mechanisms may not be working."

This is a lede from personal experience. It is something almost anyone with a 9-year-old can relate to.

Creating a powerful lede may involve adding some elements. You can mention the stakes involved to heighten interest or add a little known fact to pique your reader's curiosity.

Look at this opening statement:

"You're 475 times more likely to survive a plane crash than you are to click on a banner ad." This was first used by Business Insider, and also used by Dan Shewan in an article for WordStream.

It grabs your attention and makes you want to read more of the article. Another one is:

"An average American graduate is 4 times more likely to be unemployed in 2022."

As much as these examples look like clickbait, they are powerful catch-statements in your introduction that heighten curiosity.

- What is the Value Proposition?

This is the value you're offering the reader. Why should anyone read your article? After reading your compelling headline, the reader must see the reason to read your article.

This is why you need to state it. Let's develop one of the examples given above:

"My 9-year-old niece Ashley got her first smartphone in January. So, she can finally take goofy pictures of herself and ask Google the almost uncountable questions she asks daily.

However, one thing I have realized is that she spends a lot of time with the device, and I get worried that the age-restriction mechanisms may not be working.

I did a lot of research and I consulted tech experts, and I have been able to come up with ways to ensure that the smartphone is safe for my niece. Here are ten simple ways to ensure that the smartphone is safe for your pre-teens, and teenagers."

By telling the reader in the last paragraph that I'm going to talk about ways to ensure that the smartphone is safe for young people, I have stated the value proposition. Anyone who can resonate with the first two paragraphs will be able to resonate with the last paragraph.

The reader will want to read further to see how to guard against young folks getting exposed to adult content.

- What is the Answer to the Question You Asked in the Title?

Let's say you provided a headline like this "**Why You Should Drop Everything and Head to Thailand for a Vacation.**" Your aim should be to give the reason from the start. If you cannot answer the 'why' question, you will lose your readers.

Giving an introduction like this will help answer the question:

"With breathtaking landscapes in its Southern and Northern regions, delicious dishes, and highly hospitable people, Thailand is one of the best places to be at any time of the year. Let nature envelop you with the beautiful scenery. Easily find your calm with the gentle breeze that blows at the colorful beaches. Discover new places, and find out why tech companies are moving to Thailand in droves."

With the introduction, I have been able to answer the

question. The next thing is to let the reader know what the body of the article will be about. That's the value proposition. And in the body, you can sell a trip to Thailand.

- Use a Compelling Quote

"Blessed are the hearts that can bend; they shall never be broken." - Albert Camus

The above quote is thought-provoking. It makes you stop to think about it. You can use this at the beginning of your article.

Quotations may seem a lazy way to start an article, but they can be very effective. Not all statements become quotations, most quotations grab attention and are thought-provoking, irrespective of who said it and when.

"Any product that needs a manual to work is broken."

This statement is contrarian. When you buy an electronic product, you're expecting it to come with a manual on how it operates. You can either have it as a booklet or an e-manual. So, this statement by Elon Musk makes you want to think about it twice.

- Use Statistics or Fun Fact

About 43% of American adults are obese according to the Center for Disease Control and Prevention. This means that more than 2 in 5 American adults are obese.

This is a fact that grabs attention. One that grabs more attention is:

"One person dies every 37 seconds in the United States from cardiovascular disease. About 647,000 Americans die from heart disease each year—that's 1 in every 4 deaths."

Now, that's more attention-grabbing. Though this should not be exploited. It is useful if you're writing about heart diseases and how they can be prevented.

- Fun Fact

If you want to write an article about the dangers of artificial intelligence, you can use this fun fact introduction.

"In 2017, Facebook had to shut down two AI chatbots who could talk to each other after they created a secret language incomprehensible for human beings."

This piques the interest of many readers. It is scary when one considers the potentials of artificial intelligence and at the same time an interesting piece to read.

- Tell a Story

"Just like most 16-year-olds, Steph badly wanted to get a car and attend late-night parties. She wanted to be more attractive, and whatever was deemed cool

was what she did.

"Kylie, on the other hand, was a recluse. She wasn't interested in parties and her mom had to force her to learn how to drive. Asides streaming Netflix, she would spend hours reading her collection of Harlequin novels.

"Though twin sisters, they never really got along. They had different rooms at the age of 12 and would avoid each other at school.

"It wasn't until a family trip to the Caribbean that the twin started talking and expressing sisterly affection for each other.

That's just one of the many benefits of going on family vacations. Here are five other surprising reasons why your family needs a vacation before the year runs out."

That's an introduction telling a story. It catches your attention and makes you want to read to the end. The brain is wired to pay attention to emotional connections and triggers. Stories provide these.

We might skim a blog post, however, we would rather read a story to know what happened after the climax.

This technique has been used by many writers to draw their

readers' attention. Check out this post by Neil Patel on QuickSprout:

When you start a company, it becomes your baby, and one of the hardest things to do is let go of it.

In 2008, I started a company called KISSmetrics with my co-founder Hiten Shah. The company has grown nicely, and we raised millions of dollars to help expand the growth of the business.

But what Hiten and I never really announced was that in 2014, we left KISSmetrics. Here's why we left, and here's what's next... [click to continue...]

117 Comments   Tweet 361

Source: HubSpot

I bet you're interested in what happened after. That's the power of using stories. They compel.

- Ask an Interesting Question

"If you were given 1000 acres of land, what would you do with it?"

This is not a question that comes to mind daily. This is sure to get your attention and make you think.

There is a lot you can do with 1000 acres. You can sell it, farm on it, build a large sprawling estate on it, give it to charity, or pass it down if you have children. It is like owning a country. These are the thoughts that will fill the mind of readers.

Asking questions makes the article conversational. And if you remember when we discussed how to create a blog post, I said that writing a blog post is like having a conversation.

This conversation may appear one-sided, but while you write you can imagine the reader nodding in agreement with your points because of the way you present them.

Asking an interesting question helps you start the conversation in an interesting way.

However, you should ask a question that relates to the body of the article. You want to usher your audience into the article with this method, not just to make them read the introduction. So, in developing the question-introduction above, it will become:

"If you were given 1000 acres of land, what would you do with it?

A lot, I bet.

Now, ask yourself this: what if you had a credit card that charges no annual fee, just 10% APR, an excellent 10% cashback on all purchases, no foreign transaction fee, and no transfer fee?

Just like the 1000 acres, you can do whatever you want, spend whatever you want, and fly wherever you want. The world is without boundaries for you; earn rewards while you enjoy the beauty the world has to offer."

I have just attempted to sell a credit card using this introduction.

- Set a Scene

After trying for five years to break the glass ceiling, and the phone beeps again. It is another email from HR. This has the subject "Re: Promotion to Sales Executive Position". This is when the heart beats the fastest and the loudest. The early winter cold is still blowing, but sweat is rapidly forming on the face. This could be the best Christmas gift or another heartbreak. Clicks.

"We're sorry, but we would have preferred you if you had an MBA. All other candidates have MBAs and we couldn't pass them by. We understand you're the most experienced, but an advanced qualification is required for the office you're vying for."

You don't want to be the person in the story. You want to be armed and guarded on all sides. That's why you need an MBA. Break every glass ceiling and reach beyond the summit.

In trying to advertise an MBA degree, I set the scene. I created a scenario about a person who has been passed for a promotion because of an MBA.

Nobody wants to experience that. However, that's enough to hook a reader to read to the end of the story. And the chances that I will generate high-quality leads for the MBA institution are high.

When you set the scene, you can twist it to support a position, product, or idea. It is like telling a story. You will be able to hook the reader and manipulate some emotions to introduce what you have to offer.

This is used in normal TV commercials. Many of them take us through emotional rollercoasters and make us want to get the product almost immediately.

Ensure that the plot of the story flows and it moves towards your intended goal. Don't get provocative with the story, focus on the point you're trying to make.

Tips for an Effective Introduction

As much as there are several ways to write an introduction, there are also tips on how to make them effective.

Here are 6 tips for your introduction:

1. Use Clear and Meaningful Adjectives

If you go to the end of the previous chapter, there are 100 power words. These words are mostly adjectives. They work because they give meaning to the subject.

However, be careful with their usage. Use adjectives with clear meanings. Don't use high-sounding words that are difficult to understand. Write as if your reader is an eleven-year-old.

When choosing your adjectives, use words that will create vivid mental pictures in the mind of the reader. Words like 'all-inclusive', 'free', 'scientifically-proven', and 'easy' have inherent meanings and they paint pictures in the minds of the reader.

2. Be Concise

It is an introduction. You can say more in the body of the article. Keep it short and straight to the point. Don't forget that the reader needs the information as fast as possible. When you stall, you increase the bounce rate for the page.

In being concise, keep your sentences and paragraphs short. Even if you have about 4 - 5 paragraphs in the introduction, it will be easier to skim than a thick block of text. At most, have 4 sentences in a paragraph.

If you would have more, keep the sentences short.

3. Don't Use Generic Observations

"Paris is a beautiful city. The roads are well-paved, and at night, the city is beautifully lit."

This statement is nice, only that it is generic. I can substitute London, Oslo, Sydney, Las Vegas, and many other beautiful cities of the world for it. There is nothing unique to Paris in the statement.

You need to avoid using statements like this in your introduction. Instead, use a statement like this:

"Apart from the breathtaking Eiffel Tower on the Champs de Mars, there is so much more that adds up to the beauty of Paris."

4. Say Something Unique

Many times, readers check up to two to three posts while doing research. After giving in to the attraction of the headline, the introduction welcomes them to the article.

Now, you don't want to sound like everyone else. You want to stand out. If you sound like everyone else, the reader is just going to think there is nothing special about your article.

You should hit the article in a way that is hard to rip off. If you have tried several introductions and none works, use a story or set a scene. Stories can sell anything. You can draw from personal experience.

5. Speak to Your Reader

The pronouns 'you', 'your', and 'yours' are used in conversations. They foster engagement. When you use any of those pronouns, you are making direct communication. And communication is both ways.

Using these pronouns will help you speak to your reader. Since blog posts should be written as if you're in a conversation, you should speak to your reader.

Don't get over-dramatic with it. Just have a normal conversation. Keep a sincere and helpful tone.

6. Don't forget to mention what the article is about

As much as the title might lead to a click on the post, the reader seeks reassurance from the introduction that the article is indeed about what she needs.

This is why you should mention what the article is about in the introduction. Apart from helping to retain those interested in the topic, it prepares the reader for what is about to come in the article.

Look at this example:

6 Credit card tips for smart users

Used responsibly, a credit card can be a very helpful financial tool. Making consistent, on-time payments can boost your credit rating, and some cards offer rewards for purchases or even a 0% interest rate for a short period of time on balances transferred from other credit cards.

But if your credit spending gets out of control, monthly payments and accumulated interest can become a problem. Follow these credit card tips to help avoid common problems:

Pay attention to the second paragraph. It moves into what the article is about. Many writers fail to mention this and it can become confusing for the reader.

When your article becomes confusing, your bounce rate increases.

Conclusion

Imagine someone was moving quickly and the person glances at you for a second, what would you say to make the person stop and listen to everything else you have to say? Would you say the same thing everyone on the roadside, waiting to sell something, would say? Or you would say something attention-grabbing?

Whatever you say here is your introduction.

6. WRITING LONG-FORM ARTICLES

Reading Seth Godin's blog will make you want to become a blogger almost immediately. Who wouldn't like to write 300-word blog posts and get thousands of shares? But then, that's the seemingly easy part. The tough part is consistency.

There is hardly a day that you won't find a new post on Seth Godin's blog. And he's not repetitive. He produces unique content.

He is consistent.

However, not all blog posts can be like Godin's. You cannot write an exhaustive 300-word article on how to do on-page and off-page SEO. You need images, steps, points, and tips. You even need to give some proof that what you're saying works.

Most blog posts fall below 1000 words. This was discovered in the research of over 1 million internet articles by BuzzSumo and Moz. Look at the facts below:

Long form content consistently receives more shares and links than shorter-form content

We removed videos and quizzes from our initial sample to analyze the impact of content length. This gave us a sample of 489,128 text based articles which broke down by content length as follows:

Length (words)	No in sample	Percent
<1,000	418,167	85.5
1-2,000	58,642	12
2-3,000	8,172	1.7
3,000-10,000	3,909	0.8

Over 85% of articles had less than 1,000 words.

By this report, over 85% of articles had less than 1000 words.

Does this mean anything? It is good to know that the majority of blog posts are below 1000 words.

The effect of this comes out in post shares and traffic. The same report analyzed the share rate and backlinks for these articles and found this out:

We looked at the impact of content length on total shares and domain links.

Length (words)	Total Shares Average	Referring Domain Links Average
<1,000	2,823	3.47
1-2,000	3,456	6.92
2-3,000	4,254	8.81
3-10,000	5,883	11.07

According to the results of this research, the longer the content, the more the shares and websites linking back to it.

So, it is safe to say that one long-form content is better than 5 short content pieces. However, long-form content is not easy to create.

You can write a 500-word article in 2 to 3 hours, but a 3000-word article can take days to complete. The research alone can be grueling. However, you need them.

How to Write Long-form Articles (3000+ words)

1. What Do You Want to Write About?

This is where it starts - knowing what you want to write. You may be able to ramble for 300 - 500 words, but you can't do that for 3000 words. You must have a specific goal you want to accomplish.

- How Unique is it?

  This is a question you must be able to answer well enough. There is no point in writing exactly what someone else has written. Find a unique angle you can approach the subject from. Even if someone else has written on it, give it a unique voice.

  Do more research to expand it; make it more simple and present it in a more attractive way.

- Find Current Ideas with Google Trends

  Google Trends is where you can get what is being searched the most at a particular time. It gives a list of trending searches at any particular time. You can restrict your search to a particular time frame.

  You can do some keyword research with Google Trends to see the rate at which the keyword is searched. This can help you decide if there is some search interest in what you're about to write on.

- Is it Evergreen?

  Simply put, evergreen content is a piece of content that is as useful in six months as it is on the day it is published.

  This means that the content must be useful whenever

it is accessed. A piece of content like "**Facebook Marketing in 2014: Here's Everything You Need to Know**" will not be useful after 2014. It is not evergreen.

See the image below for what constitutes evergreen content:

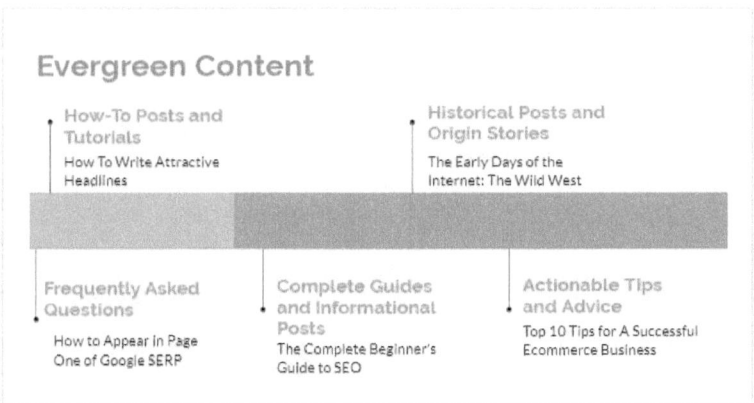

2. The Place of Extensive Research

For an article of 1200+, you need to know what you're talking about. This is why you need to do your research. Even if you're an expert, you need newer pieces of information and different perspectives on the issue.

- Find Resource Pages

  A resource page is a page on a website that contains helpful links and resources for a particular topic. Blogs use these pages to get backlinks to their content.

However, getting listed is not as easy as it looks. The content must be indeed valuable and it must be on the topic.

These requirements make them highly useful for research. And you can easily get resource pages on Google.

To get resource pages, you need to use search strings. Here's a list of them:

- ❏ Keyword + "resources"
- ❏ Keyword + "useful resources"
- ❏ Keyword + "helpful resources"
- ❏ Keyword + "links"
- ❏ Keyword + "useful links"
- ❏ Keyword + "helpful links"

Let's take the first one:

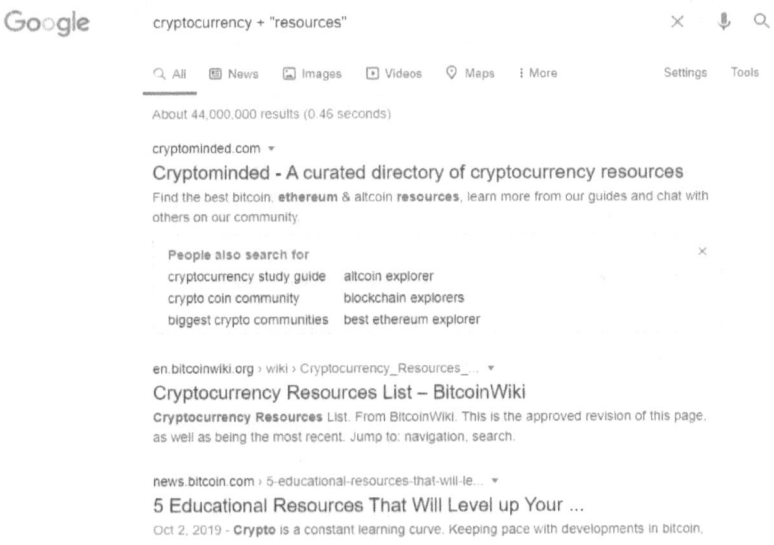

This Google Search result page gives links to resources pages on cryptocurrency. Let's pick the first one:

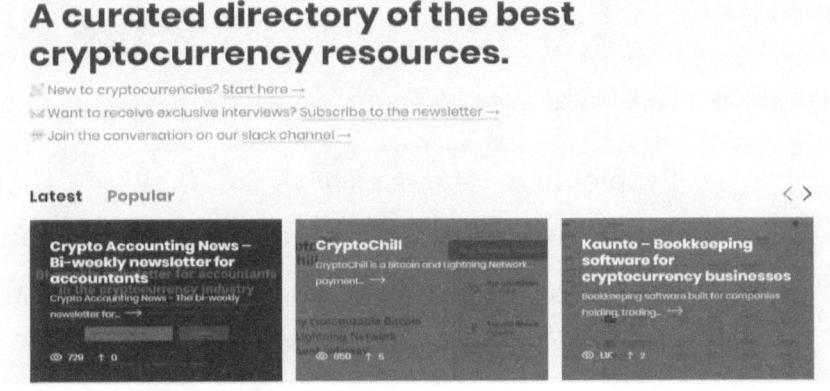

And this page still features other helpful resource directories.

So, you can start your research here.

- Don't Trust Everything on Wikipedia

Wikipedia is great, especially if you're new to a concept. You can find a ton of resources on Wikipedia. However, anyone could have written what you're reading. You're not sure about the authoritativeness of the source of the fact established. The writer can also be largely ignorant of the concept.

Even Wikipedia has this to say:

- Get Data, Lots of Them

  People like figures. They like to know that about 70% of American adults use Facebook. To increase the rate of people linking back to your work, you need a data-backed article.

  Apart from the fact that it appeals to the reader, it increases trust in your work. It shows you conducted extensive research.

  If you pay attention to traditional marketing,

you get to hear things like "9 in 10 moms recommend this product." This invariably increases interest in the product.

- Use Google Scholar for Academic Articles

Google Scholar gives you access to millions of academic articles. In certain niches like health, citing academic research papers and reports will give your article more weight. This is what Healthline does.

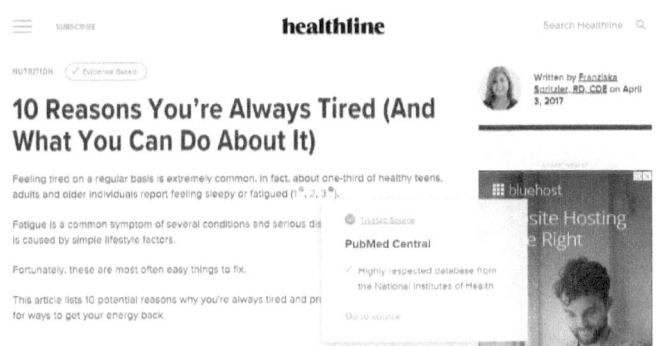

Look at that part that says "Trusted Source" and cites PubMed Central. If you click on it, you will be taken to an academic paper. It is no surprise that Healthline comes first or second in Google search results.

To access Google Scholar, go to scholar.google.com, and input your keyword.

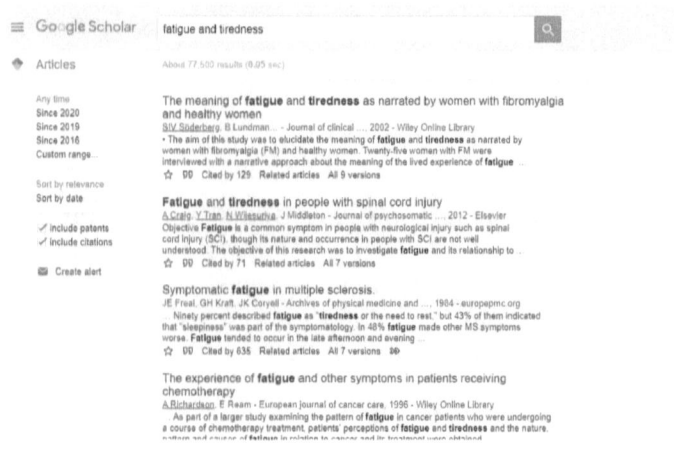

3. Outline

Without an outline, what you're meant to write in 12 hours, you may write it in 24 hours. Outlining your work helps you to give it a structure and this invariably saves you time. You don't start to think about what to write next, you already know.

Having a structure makes your work easy to read. You have major points and subheadings. It is easy for the reader who wants to scan the article for information.

To outline, you can use Google Documents or any word processor of choice. Many digital marketers find Evernote to be very useful for this. Here is an outline created by Michael Hyatt of Coschedule on Evernote:

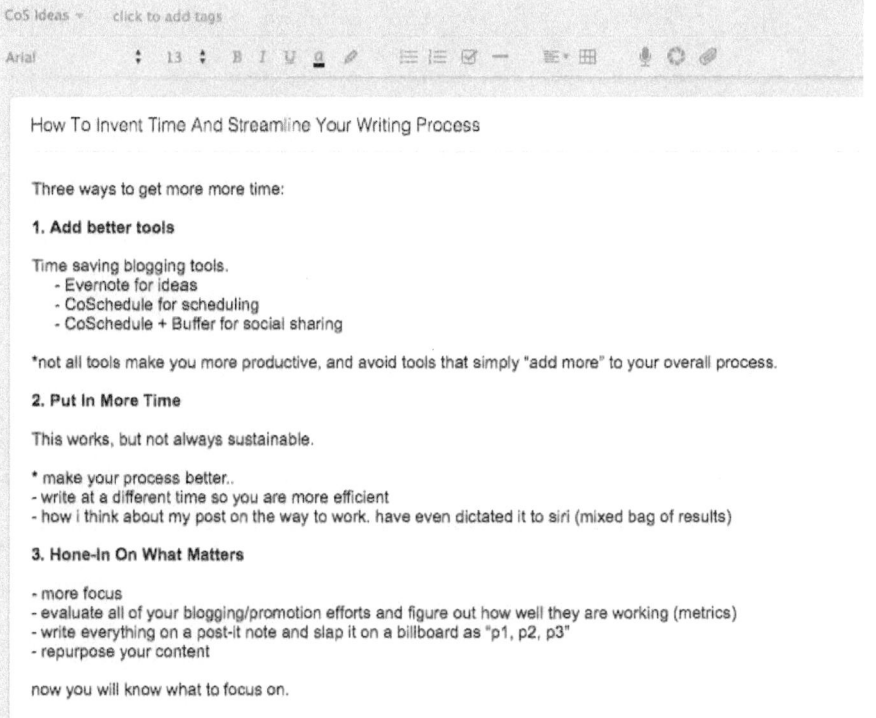

4. Edit Later

Many writers make the mistake of editing while writing. It is normal to have those errors; the best of us make mistakes. However, you should correct the errors later.

When writing, you should let the words flow without interruptions. At that point, your mind is full of what to say. Disrupting the flow can make you forget what you are about to say or how you want to say it.

Experienced bloggers advise that you write everything you have in your mind to write and edit when you're done.

5. Short Sentences and Paragraphs and Be Mindful of SEO

I cannot overemphasize the importance of keeping your sentences and paragraphs short. As I have repeatedly said, write as if your reader is an eleven-year-old.

Even if you're an expert, don't assume your readers will also be experts. Write as if your readers are beginners. The truth is that most experts won't read your work. They conduct new experiments or look for those conducted by others.

When it comes to sentences, don't do more than 20 words. If you would in exceptional cases, let it be a few. Sentences with fewer words are easy to read.

When you have long sentences, use punctuation correctly. They help to make your article more comprehensible.

For sentences, don't do more than 4 sentences at the most in a paragraph. Look at Jon Morrow's article:

The painful truth about why you can't be yourself

It's because you're inhibited, dearie.

All of us are, to one degree or another, and thank God. Can you imagine what the world would be like if we acted on every impulse to pass through our little heathen brains?

Why, it would be a mess. People would be fornicating in church, passing out drunk in the wine aisle of the grocery store, murdering their children for failing to take out the garbage, and God only knows what else.

To protect ourselves from such ill-advised behavior, we all learn during childhood that there are Angels and Demons within all of us, and if we are to survive, we must encourage the former and discourage the latter. Or else.

Apart from the fact that the paragraphs are short, the article is well-spaced. White spaces help to make online content more attractive to read.

Jon Morrow is the CEO of Smart Blogger and he is one of the most respected bloggers in Content Marketing.

Other tips under this point are:

- Optimize for SEO

  As you write, have SEO in mind. It is much easier to write an SEO-optimized article from scratch than optimize an already-written article.

  When you have your keywords or focus keyphrase before you start writing, you will be able to use it naturally in the article. It is even advisable that some of your upper subheadings carry your keywords or focus keyphrase.

In optimizing for SEO, having subheadings is important. This can only be perfectly done when you have SEO in mind when writing.

You need internal and external links to be properly optimized for SEO. Internal links are links to articles within your website. External links are the links to the sites you got your facts and resources from. This is known as backlinking - linking back to them.

- Don't Be Constrained by the Rules of Grammar

You're not writing an academic article. So, you should not be scared of breaking certain rules of grammar. As long as what you're saying does not impact the meaning or comprehensiveness of the statement, you're good.

Look at this example from Jon Morrow's article*:

"To protect ourselves from such ill-advised behavior, we all learn during childhood that there are Angels and Demons within all of us,

and if we are to survive, we must encourage the former and discourage the latter. Or else."

The last sentence is grammatically incorrect. A sentence should contain a verb, at the very least. Neither of "or" or "else" is a verb.

However, the sentence makes perfect sense when considered in the context of the whole paragraph.

- Use Table of Content

A table of content helps the reader navigate the content easily. Apart from that, it makes it easy to know what the article is about. Check out this table of content by Brian Dean of Backlinko:

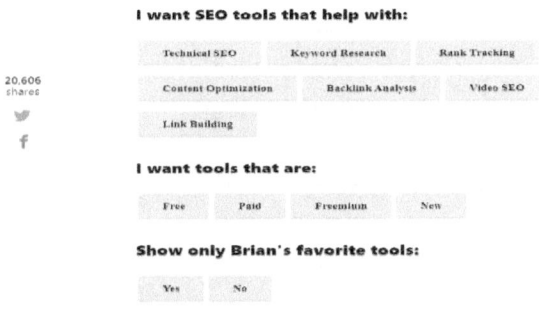

All you need to do is click on the particular aspect you want, check if you want a paid or free tool, and decide between Brian's favorite or not. And that's all you will get.

If you want to go through all the tools, just read on.

This is highly innovative. You can use some plugins to help you with this. WordPress has the Table of Content Plus plugin.

6. Use Original Images, Cartoons, or Animations

The human brain processes image 60,000 times faster than it does text.

The thing about images is that they attract. They help you break your work into more comprehensive bits. And one picture can tell a thousand words.

Getting images can be simple and, at the same time, difficult. If you only have to use a picture with someone making a facial expression, you can easily get stock photos for that.

However, if you need something designed, it can cost you. Animations and cartoons can also be expensive. This is because professionals are paid to create them.

Look at this picture:

Credits: Anastacia Bankulova - Pixabay

This kind of picture is not something you can easily get on a stock website. This is good for fashion, but what if you are writing about health, investment, or something else?

You need a picture that is related to what you're talking about.

- Some writers use cartoons, and they work. They can entertainingly pass messages across. Look at this:

Credits: The Telegraph

- Some writers also use memes to pass their messages across in an entertaining way. However, you want to be careful with the kind of content you use memes on. It is not advisable to use memes for B2B content because of their professional nature.

  For B2C content, it works well. Check out this meme:

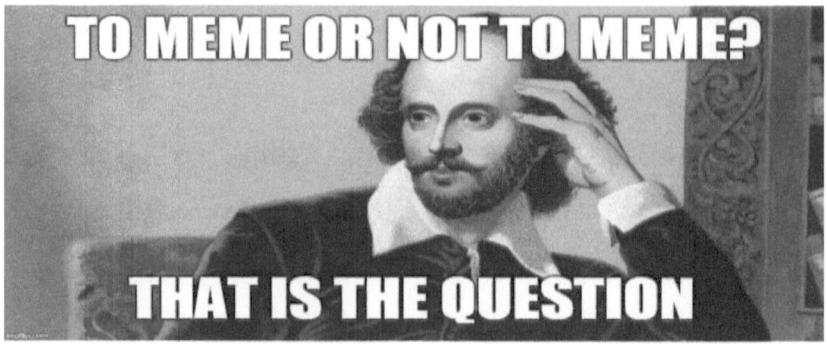

- Screenshots

Screenshots work very well when you're trying to prove a point. You can take the screenshot of a graph, a report, or anything. Screenshots have been used extensively in this book to make certain concepts more comprehensible.

To add text and other details to your screenshot, you can use a tool like Skitch. It will do the screenshot and make it editable with its features.

- Stock Photos and Royalty-free Images

The thing about stock images, especially free ones, is that you're most likely not the only person using it. A lot of other people have them in their blogs.

What you can do is to edit it and add some text. Since crediting is optional, you can still edit. However, when you can, credit the author and link back.

You can get royalty-free photos from Pixabay, Unsplash, Pexels, and many others.

- Amateur Photos

You may find it hard to believe, but amateur photos do better than stock photos, in some circumstances. In ads and blog posts, amateur photos can do a lot better.

For instance, if you own a keto blog, you want to use the pictures of real people who have found success in doing it. You don't want an edited and clean picture that someone else may be using.

More, people find it easy to believe if it is amateur. The editing isn't there and it looks real.

But then, stock photos are the most-used. This is because they can fit in several circumstances.

7. Proofread

If you remember, I said you should edit later. This is the 'later'. This is where you have to go over your work and correct all the errors.

However, refer to the next chapter for a detailed article on the several ways to proofread your work.

Conclusion

Writing long-form content is like having a long conversation. You don't want to lose the engagement and the connection the reader must feel. Use pictures to spice up the work, and ensure that there are white spaces.

Long-form content pays off and all you need is to put in the work.

When writing, your focus should not be on completing the whole article. It should be on completing an aspect well and then moving on to the next aspect.

Focus on each task at a time. When you have your outline ready, you will find it easy to fix each point or aspect of the article as a task.

7. PROOFREADING

This may seem tough when you just got off writing 2000+ words. Here are tips for proofreading your own work:

❑ Take Some Time Off

Take a break. You can even take a nap or see a movie. Clear your mind before you return to the work.

❑ Add Page Numbers

Page numbers allow you to track your work easily. You can easily get where you were and make necessary changes.

❑ Print Your Work Out

Yes, you may need to go back to the pen and paper days. Computer screens make your eyes tired easily. This is from the glare. The result of this is that you slip into skim reading.

❏ Read Slowly

Now, read your work line by line slowly. Read it aloud. Not too loud, so you don't wake your neighbors.

The thing about reading your work aloud is that what your eyes will not catch, your ears will. More, when you read a sentence and it doesn't sound good to the ears, rewrite it. Change the erring or difficult word for something easier.

❏ Put Away Distractions

This is one of the reasons why you need a break after writing. Return calls, reply emails and do whatever else you need to do. While you're proofreading, you need to fully concentrate. You can't be chatting on one hand and editing on the other.

Also, clear your mind of distracting thoughts. If you need to take another break, take it. But do one thing at a time.

❏ Work Like a Professional

A professional proofreader will have a correcting mindset. The focus will be to identify the mistakes and point them out. So, approach the work as if you're not the writer.

❏ Get Familiar with Your Frequent Mistakes

When you edit your work and over and over, you will notice

those mistakes you make constantly. Pay attention to them. Consistency is great, but when you're consistently making the same mistakes, then you're not making progress.

❏ Watch Out for Homophones

Homophones are words that sound the same but have very different meanings and origins. Take "its" and "it's". Many confuse both. Other homophones like "there", "they're", and "their" appear frequently on several blogs. These mistakes confuse the reader.

❏ Fact-Check

Numbers, dates, and figures draw attention. You don't want to give inaccurate information. I once made the mistake of writing "Twitter has 300 billion monthly active users." instead of "Twitter has 300 million monthly active users." It was a very slippery one. If it had not been found out, it would have been published like that. And that would have reduced the credibility of the 2500+ word article.

❏ Check Your Formatting Last

Let this come last. Check for punctuations, spellings, SEO, and grammatical errors first.

Here are commonly-used tools you can use to check your work:

- **Grammarly**

For Grammarly, you should get the Chrome extension and the desktop app. You can also head to the website to use the online editor.

If you're working in Google Docs or WordPress Text Editor, Grammarly will flag your errors. Though you need a premium version to enjoy all the features.

- **Hemingway Editor**

Patterned after Ernest Hemingway's simple style of writing, the goal of the Hemingway Editor is to have simple and easy-to-understand articles.

Hemingway checks your readability. It sets the standard to the level of a Grade 6 student. That's why I advocate writing for the comprehension of an eleven-year-old.

Your word usage, the length of your sentences, the use of

passive words, and other factors will be checked. Your sentences will be flagged when they contradict readability standards. Check the interface out:

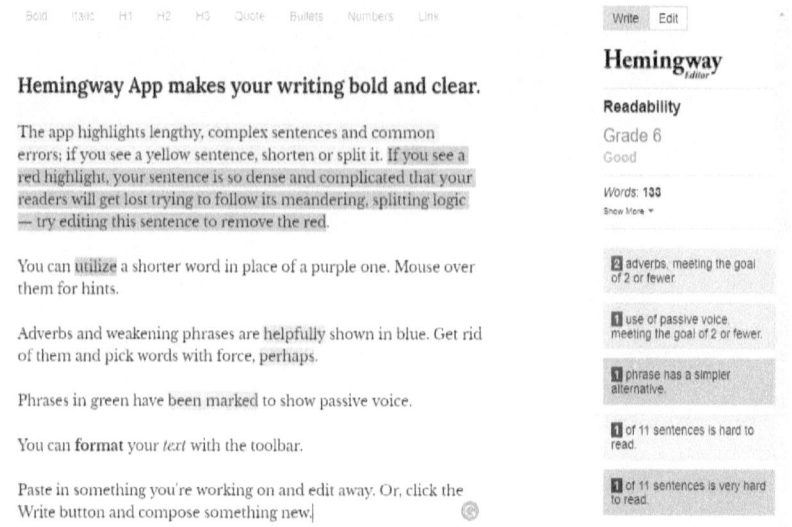

- Yoast SEO

Yoast SEO is another tool that helps with readability. Yoast SEO has the primary goal of optimizing your article for search engines. But then, readability is a factor when it comes to SEO. You want to provide a smooth experience to every visitor that reads the article.

Yoast SEO is a plugin. Though it works for other website platforms, it is known majorly for WordPress.

When you put your work in the WordPress text editor, the plugin analyzes it for SEO and readability.

It then provides you with a list of what to do and even highlights where you need to make corrections. It checks for the length of sentences and paragraphs, the difficulty of the words used, the use of connectives, and so many other factors that make for a good reading experience.

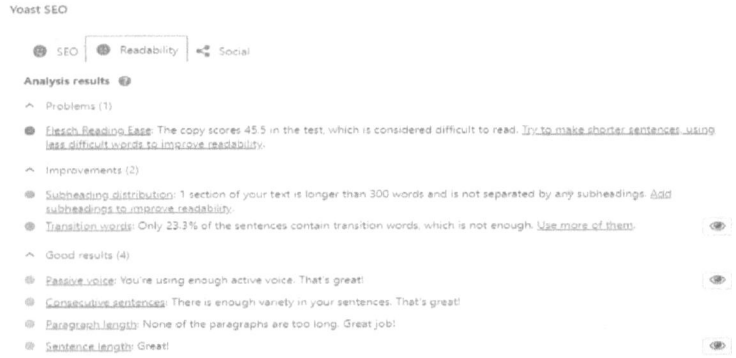

Yoast SEO has a free version and a premium version. Most bloggers use the free version because if you can check green on both SEO and Readability, it can get you to page one of Google.

- Get an Editor

If you're not confident about editing the work yourself, give it to someone whose capabilities you are confident about.

Let the person be strict with your work. This is what normal editors would do.

You may need to remove some things or rewrite some

paragraphs, but it will be worth it in the end.

You can get freelance editors online or ask someone you know to do it for you. There are freelance editors on Upwork, Fiverr, Freelancer, and many other platforms online. This will cost you but you should be able to get a freelancer to work within a small budget.

Conclusion

Most writers don't like to proofread their writings. The brain can easily fill the spots at which mistakes are made. This means you may not know you made a mistake. However, with the tips given above, you will be able to proofread your work.

As much as you feed your work to online tools such as Grammarly and Hemingway Editor, you should still read the work over. Their suggestions aren't always perfect.

8. WRITING FOR SEO

The other titles I would have loved to give to this chapter are: "How to Write Articles Attractive to Search Engines" and "How to Get on Page One of Google".

Notwithstanding, the goal of this chapter is to teach you how to write well-optimized blog posts and articles. And I will teach you this in the simplest way I can.

Let's start:

What is SEO?

SEO is search engine optimization. It basically means optimizing a piece of content to enable its visibility to search engines.

Search engine algorithms are smart robots who have been programmed to recognize certain features and rank based on those features.

To rank means to give a website a position in relation to a particular search term. So, if your article is about finding the best love partner, your article will be ranked based on certain factors which include how well-optimized is your article for the keyword or focus keyphrase.

You need to know that there are two aspects to SEO - on-page SEO and off-page SEO.

On-page SEO is what we shall deal with in detail in this chapter. Off-page SEO includes link building and domain authority. We shall deal with an aspect of it that involves backlinks.

Here are things and tips you should know to rank well

1. Keyword or Focus Keyphrase

This is the search intent you want to rank for. The way Google works is that when a user runs a search, the algorithm runs through the indexed pages and looks for those with keywords inline with the search term.

So, if I search 'how to keep my heart healthy', Google's search algorithm will search all its indexed pages to look for those optimized for 'heart healthy', 'keep heart healthy', 'ways to keep the heart healthy'.

Pages optimized for these keywords will appear in the search results.

So, this is where your keyword or focus keyphrase comes in.

Before you set out to write, you must do your keyword research. This means you go out to see what people are searching - the intent of people while searching for something relating to what you are writing about.

So, if I want to write about 'how to keep my heart healthy', I need to run a search on Google and see the suggestions I'm given.

Those suggestions are not manufactured by Google, they are what people really search for. They show the intent of people in relation to that keyword. Look at this:

What you need to do is to take the suggestions related to

your keyword or focus keyphrase and sprinkle them in the first few paragraphs of your article.

You can get more focused suggestions at the end of the search results page. Here:

When you're sprinkling these suggestions, let them flow naturally with the article. Take "healthy heart exercises" (one of the suggestions), I will need to write something like:

"One of the ways to keep your heart healthy is to engage in healthy heart exercises regularly. Cardiologists recommend this."

- The Appropriate Use of Keywords

Many writers think that the more keywords appear in a piece of content, the more visible it is. That's no longer the case.

Recent updates to the Google algorithm have revealed that it goes beyond having keywords. In fact, overusing keywords - keyword stuffing - is a blackhat practice that can attract the wrath of the 'mighty Google'. You can get sanctioned for it.

For an article of 1000 words, your keyword or focus keyphrase should appear just 4 - 6 times. They should appear mostly in the early part of the content.

For 2000 words, the keyword or focus keyphrase appearing 8 times is good enough.

Ensure that the keyword or focus keyphrase is naturally written into the article.

- Latent Semantic Indexing (LSI) Keywords

Like I said earlier, the Google algorithm is an intelligent robot. It gets smarter with time. There was a time when only the keywords really mattered. Now, It has been programmed to understand intentions.

For instance, the word "car" has different meanings.

➢ Cars - vehicles
➢ Cars - The Pixar animation movie "Cars"
➢ The Cars - late 1970s American rock band

So, the search for the word "cars" may seem confusing to the algorithm and it will just produce pages well-optimized for it.

However, Google relies on the modifiers to understand the search intent. So, if I refine my search and enter "Cars 3" or "Cars movie". The Google algorithm knows I'm searching for the Pixar animation movie.

Look at it:

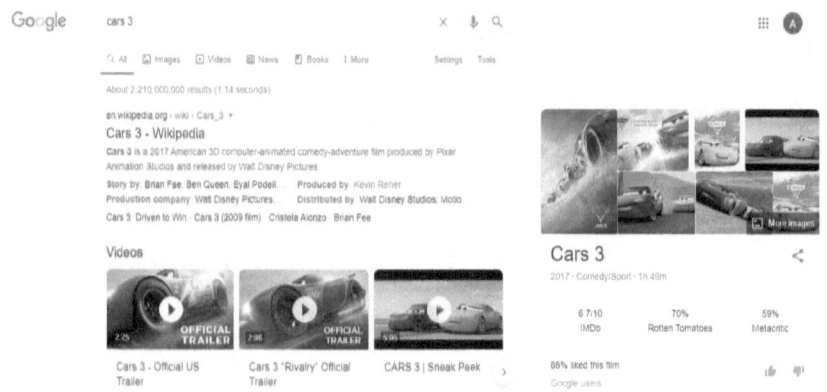

For the American rock band, I just need to include "band" or "rock" after the word "cars" and Google will return with results exactly matching the band. Here is it:

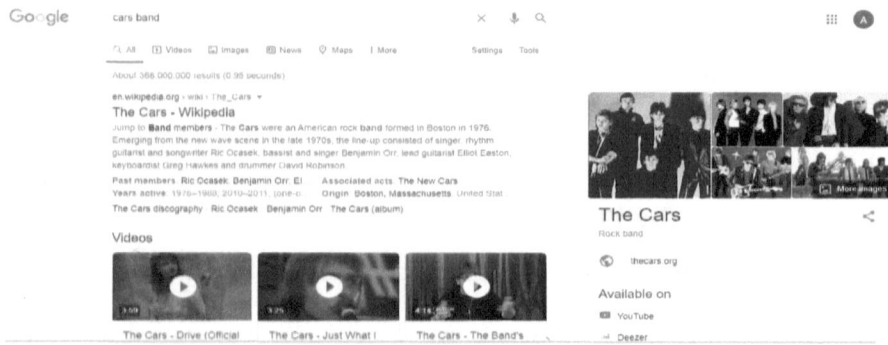

Since the Google algorithm will be looking out for modifiers to give contextual meanings to the keyword, you will be doing yourself a lot of good to anticipate this.

Instead of just writing "cars" and hoping to rank for it, use modifiers and related words in your copy (article). Look at this:

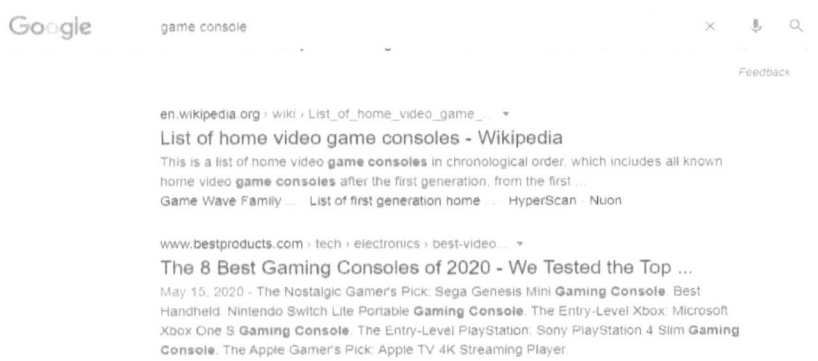

The pages that ranked for the Cars band used words and phrases that are related to it. This can help you rank better than many other pages not doing this.

Before you start writing, run a search for the keyword, and see related words to it. The search for "game console" on Google brought this:

Notice that some words are in bold lettering, these are words related to game consoles. These words also have modifiers like "video game consoles", "portable gaming console", "slim gaming console".

You should sprinkle these around your article. Use them naturally to help your content rank better.

- Keyword Research in Forums

Forums are one great place to do keyword research. In forums, people ask the questions that really bother them. If you're looking for what to write on or a common term, you should stalk forums.

To get forums on a particular subject, enter: inurl: forums + "keyword".

For instance, inurl: forums + "dogs"

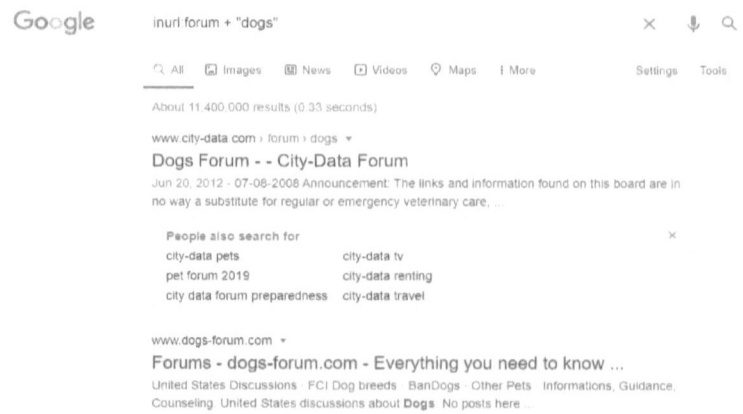

You choose a forum and read the discussions.

Take a look at this forum. The discussion is on neutering.

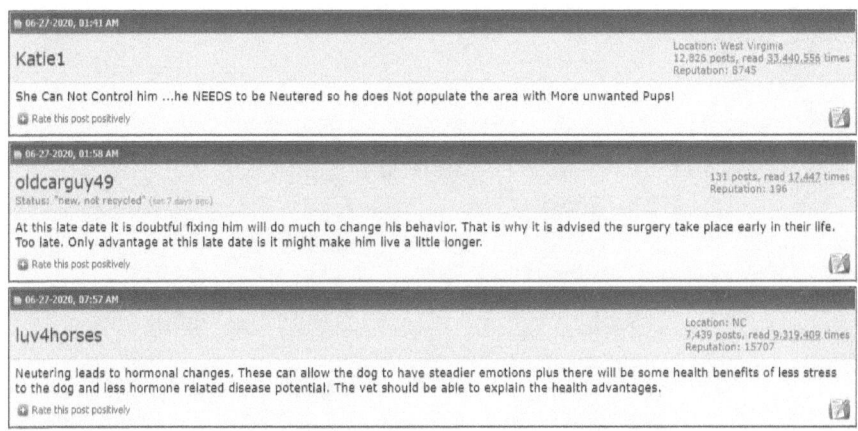

From the third discussion, I can choose to write on the dangers of failing to neuter a dog at an early age.

- Keywords in Headings and Slugs

Your headings and slugs will help you rank better if they contain your keywords or focus keyphrase.

If your keyword or focus keyphrase is "how to build a sandcastle", you should have a headline like:

"10 Simple and Fun Ways to Build Breathtaking Sand Castles"

Or "7 Easy Steps to Build an Epic Sand Castle"

Look at this:

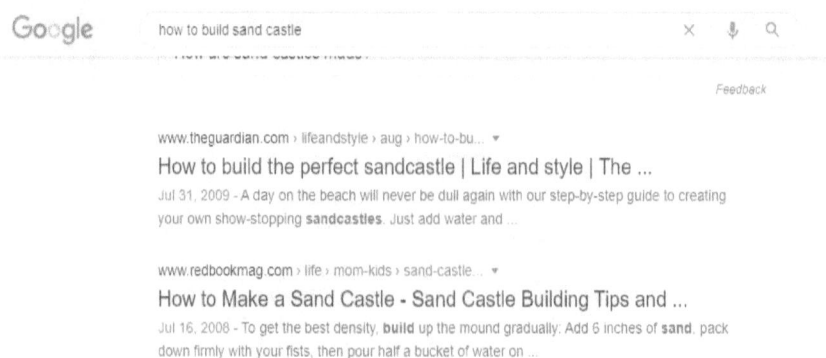

The fact that the title contains the keyphrase not only makes it rank but also attractive to the internet user. It clearly bears the intent of the internet user.

The slug is the latter part of the URL. Look at this:

https://wokenliving.com/woken/best-cryptocurrency/

The "best-cryptocurrency" is the slug and it also happens to be the focus keyphrase of the article.

Using the keyword in the slug helps to tell the search algorithm what your article is about. And, keep it short. You don't want it containing unnecessary items like dates and figures.

2. Subheadings

They matter to SEO.

Posts with lists are best for SEO ranking. Google loves them. This is because people can easily get what they are looking for.

Telling people '10 ways to get something done' is more attractive than just blocks of text on getting it done.

When you do this, you need to format your subheadings well. No subheading should be more than 300 words.

You format by using 'H' tags. 'H' tags are heading tags. If you're writing on a word processor, here is what you need to do.

Just highlight the subheading and head to 'styles' in your word processor, click on 'Heading 2' if it is a major subheading like a point or step in a post like '5 Steps to Becoming Awesome'.

Each step is a subheading.

Now, if you have a smaller subheading. Let's say in one step 'Be More Appreciative of People', you have something like 'How to be more appreciative'. You will use 'Heading 3' or 'H3'. If that also has another subheading, you will use 'Heading 4' or 'H4'.

You need to be consistent with the headings. Major points have the same headings.

In the WordPress text editor, you can fix the subheading easily. This is also possible in Google Docs.

3. Use Bucket Brigades

This is a content trick to keep people on a page for longer. The thing is: when people spend less than 5 seconds on your page, you will lose ranking. This is because the Google algorithm studies behavior. Through machine learning, it notices that when people leave as soon as they land on the page, that means the page is not good.

Stop showing the page to people.

So, to counter that, bucket brigades come in handy. Here's an example:

"Do you want to know the number one secret of making it on the internet?

This secret has been kept close, and you must pay attention to what I am about to tell you.

Look:

All the courses and seminars you have been attending may have been telling you the wrong thing.

Why? You may ask.

Because they want you to keep buying.

I have made 20 million dollars in the past three years, so I know what I am talking about.

And the secret is,

The number one secret to making it on the internet.

It is simply something you would not believe.

Something we relate to every day.

And, what is it?

A five-letter word they are not spelling to you.

The secret is trust. TRUST."

If you pay attention, they have kept you longer for more than 5 seconds. If you are no longer interested, you can go. It won't affect that ranking.

The code here is to break down your work in short sentences and paragraphs and to keep the reader in anticipation of what you have to say. What would have been muddled together in a paragraph or two would be spread into 6 to 7 paragraphs.

Look at the way Brian Dean of Backliko used it here:

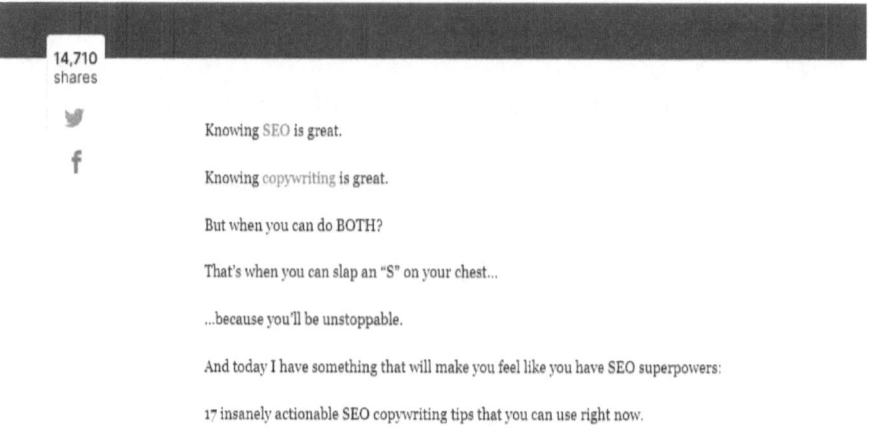

4. Use Outbound Links

Linking to other websites is not only good practice, but it is also good for SEO. You need to be linked to before you rank, it is only fair you link to other helpful resources.

An SEO tool like Yoast SEO will flag your work for not containing any external links. External links prove that you did your research. They can get where you got a fact from.

Don't only link to external sites, link to articles within your website. When the search engines crawl the page, it will help other pages rank.

5. Meta Description

If you run your blog or website, you need to always meta description. This is just a sentence or two attracting people to your piece. It must contain the focus keyphrase or keyword. The meta description is what you see after the headline in Google search results.

Here is an example:

In Yoast SEO, you have a part where you can edit the meta description. If none is found, the search engine might just pull the first few lines from your text and it may not look nice. And this can impact your traffic negatively.

Conclusion

Search engines bring the biggest traffic. You want to have hundreds of thousands of reads or visitors. Only search engines can really give that. This is why you need to understand how they work and ensure that your work is visible.

Do your keyword research and ensure that you use keywords or focus keyphrases appropriately.

9. COPYWRITING THAT CONVERTS

Imagine a world where the open rate for your email marketing is about 80%.

Also, imagine a world where everybody that gets to your landing page has no reason not to click on the call-to-action.

Both are possible when you write copies that trigger responses from your readers.

The Situation

An average person sees 5000 ads a day. Banner ads, social media marketing, billboards, posters, emails, physical mails, newspapers and magazine ads, TV commercials,... the list is almost endless.

Expectedly, the average consumer has learned to shut out marketing noise.

How then will the marketer sell?

Four ways:

- Grab attention
- Connect
- Communicate
- Call to action

These four ways work whether you're writing a web copy or an email copy.

1. Grab Attention

In your web or email copy, the headline or the subject line determines, up to 80%, if people are going to read your copy.

Do it right, and you make sales. Do it badly, and all the work in the copy wastes away.

That's how cruel it has become.

David Ogilvy, the Father of Modern Advertising said:

"If you haven't done 80% of your selling in the headline, you have wasted your client's money."

Well, in this case, it may be your money, but you have wasted 80% of it because people aren't going to read your copy.

How to Write Headlines and Subject Lines That Grab Attention

- Refer to your reader

  "To Men Who Want to Quit Work Someday"

  That's a headline written by John Caples. This headline stands out for two things: it is direct and it arouses curiosity.

  Let's use the structure to draw out an example:

  "To Email Marketers Who Want Higher Open Rates"

  Another one: "To Women Tired of Frustrating Weight Loss Efforts"

  The catch about this is that it defines its audience and strikes a subject of interest. These elements help it increase curiosity and will trigger opening the email or reading the body.

- Personalize the subject line

  Email marketing has made it very easy to sell to the prospect. You can customize the subject line to include the name of the prospect.

  Email marketing services allow you to add the name. Why not do it?

Don't forget that marketing is about the prospect. When I see a subject like this:

"John, This New Marketing Automation Software is For You"

Now, I'm curious. What is it about the software that it will be for me? And what benefits does the new software have? These are questions that would play in my mind if I got something like this.

- Include your selling promise in the headline

  "John, Get More Leads for Less With This Facebook Marketing Tool"

  Now, there is a selling promise in the headline. I'm interested because I am a digital marketer. And, I will appreciate getting more leads for less.

- Appeal to Self-Interest

  If you study the last example, you will notice that the marketer appealed to my self-interest.

  "John, Get More Leads for Less With This Facebook Marketing Tool"

  My self-interest is to get more for less.

  I will not open an email that says:

"Yayyy!!!! We've Rebranded Our Website"

Okay. What is in for me? I don't have the time to start admiring your website. That's your business. Deal with it.

Always answer the question "what's in it for me?" in the subject line.

Human beings are naturally selfish. Appeal to that base instinct.

- Use triggers words like "New" and "Free"

"Free" will send a spike to your read-through-rate and open-rate. People love free things, especially from a valuable source.

Using the word "Free" in the subject line will work miracles.

The thing about "New" is that it evokes curiosity. It makes you want to know what the new addition is.

- How-To Subject Lines

They work well.

"How Women Over 35 Can Look Younger"

"How to Get Do-Follow Backlinks with Medium"

People want helpful information. As long as you have made a move with your headline or subject line to provide it, people will want to read it.

- Keep it simple

Understand that you've got less than 3 seconds to grab attention; don't waste the time with some hard-to-understand-yet-big words. Using simple everyday words.

David Ogilvy wrote that the housewives who made most of the household shopping decisions didn't understand the big words used in some commercials. The situation hasn't changed.

People don't have the time to grab the dictionary. When the syllable is becoming unending, use a simpler word or phrase.

Also, avoid the use of flowery language. If your thing is flowery language, go and write Elizabethan drama or poetry in some art school. Leave marketers to use simple words.

- Don't use negatives

David Ogilvy gave an example:

"Our Salt Contains No Ascernic"

As innocent as this example looks, the eyes can easily skip the "No". To avoid this, avoid the use of negatives.

The example could be better written as:

"Our Salt is Arsenic-Free"

- Avoid the use of blind headlines or subject lines

  "Healthier Living

  How I Dropped 30 Pounds in a Month"

  Headlines get this the most. People see the big heading, but will hardly see the smaller one.

  The big heading evokes no curiosity. And that is what people see mostly.

  Be straight and direct with it.

- These words grab attention

  How-to, Suddenly, New, Announcing, Introducing, Just Arrived, Important development, Improvement, Amazing, Sensational, Remarkable, Revolutionary, Startling, Miracle, Magic, Offer, Quick, Easy, Wanted, Simple, Challenge, Advice to, The truth about, Compare, Bargain, Hurry, Last Chance.

- For emails, you've got about 10 words to work your magic. Don't waste it.

Rewrite your headlines or subject lines several times before you use it.

Upworthy makes it writers write about 25 headlines.

Ogilvy would write about 16.

Know that there is always a better one.

2. Connect

This is your introduction. You have succeeded in getting the reader's attention. However, don't celebrate yet.

This is where you welcome the reader. Here, no one rule fits all.

You can use a picture or a statement.

If you're writing an email, personalize.

"Hi, John" is a good way to start.

If you're using a picture, ensure that it grabs attention and evokes curiosity.

If you're using an introductory statement, set the reader's imagination in motion. Look at this:

> Imagine controlling all your social media marketing in a single dashboard. You can easily monitor ads on Facebook and see how viral your post is going on TikTok. All your login details are secured and encrypted. And you can easily share posts among

your social media platforms without wasting time.

This introduction will grab the attention of a digital marketer.

Here are a few things you should take note of here:

- Brevity: cut out fluff words. Keep your sentences short. Your first sentence should not be more than 11 words to allow for easy reading. You don't want your reader to bounce off in the first line.

  Normal sentences should not be more than 20 words. Brevity here does not extend to the length of the copy. That's dictated by the product and the benefits it has to offer.

  Keep your paragraphs short.

- Focus: as much as you're trying to paint a picture, don't go off the trail. Focus on the goal. Your goal is to sell.

  Though some marketers find success by sharing personal stories in the introduction. Nick Stephenson of WSJ Books does this well. He shares snippets of his life as a stay-at-home dad.

  > Hey John
  >
  > It's been another rather long seven days over here at Chez Stephenson, but with the new week brings a newfound sense of optimism.

> We also finally managed to get into something vaguely resembling a routine, including taking the kids out on impromptu "field trips".
>
> ("Field trips" being parenting slang for "leaving them in the woods so we can sleep").

He then takes you into the subject of the email:

> With this - perhaps misplaced - feeling of good cheer, I've decided to dedicate next month to covering everything you need to know (and do) to start bringing in a reliable income from books.

- Ask Questions: what did you have for breakfast? You most likely stopped to think about the meal you had. That's the power of asking questions. Questions engage the reader. You're hitting on their pain point by asking questions you know they would normally answer yes to. Take a look at this:

> Are you engaged in a system that is not working optimally? Do you feel like there is more you could be doing with your time? Do you strongly feel that you're worth more than what you're currently getting?

The trick is to get your prospect to nod at least three times. By understanding the pain points, you can ask questions that strike deep into their desires. Pick your questions carefully to ensure that the answers your prospect will give will be 'yes'.

3. Communicate

Yes, you have been communicating, but this is where you do the bulk of it.

Ogilvy's analogy comes to mind here. He said:

> Pretend you're talking to the woman on your right at a dinner party. She has asked 'I'm thinking of buying a new car'. Write your copy as if you're answering that question.

Let's assume you're a car sales rep. How will you answer?

- Features tell; benefits sell; facts sell better

  Telling me that a car has a V8 engine might not mean anything to me. It will mean something to a car enthusiast, but I'm lost on the technical term.

  However, telling me that I will get more performance and power in terms of speed and engine power gets me interested.

  You should list every fact of the product and let the prospect know the benefit of each fact about the product brings.

  For instance, if you're writing about a product or service that will save your prospect money, calculate precisely how much the savings will be. Let the prospect know this.

- List the facts with pictures

  Since you're going to talk about facts, do it with pictures. Pictures draw more attention. One can tell a thousand words.

  Use attractive colors, and ensure every text in the picture is legible enough.

  It is helpful to use numbers and bullets points to break your points, steps, and benefits. It also makes it easy to read.

- Go straight to the point

  This is where you do your sales pitch. You need to be on point. Don't move away from the goal. Keep hammering on the benefits and the gains of the product.

  Avoid analogies of "just as" or "so too". They are used for comparison. Unless you're comparing two products or the improvement in the one you're offering, avoid words that say "here's another option."

- Avoid generalizations

  You're selling a particular product, be specific about it. Be factual and tell the truth.

  When you generalize, it gives the impression that you

don't know much about the product. Using a previous example, I would want to know more about the performance potential of a particular car, and not about cars with V8 engines.

- Don't be boring

Like Ogilvy said: tell the truth, but make the truth fascinating. If the car has only 5 benefits, tell them in a way that will make me want to place an order immediately.

In what is known as David Ogilvy's greatest ad copy, he described the seats in the Rolls Royce this way:

> The seats are upholstered with eight hides of English leather - enough to make 128 pairs of soft shoes.

A person who can't imagine how eight hides of English leather will be can imagine sitting on what will make 128 pairs of soft shoes.

That makes it very fascinating.

- The more the qualities to describe, the longer the copy

People give the excuse that internet readers are lazy and they wouldn't read long copies. That's not true.

If you're about to put $500 upwards on a product, you will want to know everything there is to know about it.

Even if it is cheaper than $500.

Your focus should be on how to make the long copy fascinating and engaging.

When a product has more qualities, tell each quality in the best way you can. Use pictures when you can, and focus on how it benefits the user.

It is a sales pitch, tell more facts. And use imageries to paint pictures while you're telling the facts.

So, the length of the copy depends on the products you're selling. You can't sell a computer the same way you would sell a shaving stick.

- Don't use drawings

You're not selling art, you're selling a product. Don't use cartoons or drawings. Use realistic pictures of the product.

Take nice and clean shots of the product.

If it is an office item, put it in an office setting when you take the pictures. You want to give the prospect a picture of how the product will be when bought.

- Use testimonials

This is why beta-testing works. Before the product is

launched, the testimonials of beta-testers can be gathered for marketing.

Testimonials are social proofs. They give your marketing more credibility. It now goes beyond your words.

As much as celebrity endorsement is great, the testimonials of everyday people do better.

- Give helpful advice

When you constantly sell to people, they can get fatigued and your open-rate or read-through rate may drop.

Give helpful advice. Tell them 5 ways to do something easier. Provide links to helpful resources, and, while you do this, pitch your product.

You have fulfilled your end by providing the helpful advice you promised. Who says you can't sell?

- Just as it has been said *countless times* in this book, avoid flowery language.

Use short sentences and paragraphs. Avoid words that break the jaw and write as if you're talking to a friend. Keep it highly personal.

You can use everyday language and colloquialism.

Using words like *wanna, gonna, ...* are nice. You should keep it informal.

- Don't leave room for *"what-ifs"*

When you're writing your copy, list all possible objections people can have and answer them. Look at this:

> Email marketing gives room for busy people like stay-at-home parents who only have little time to focus on work.

Objections like 'I'm busy, I'm a stay-at-home parent, I don't really have time to focus on work' have been answered.

When you're selling a product, this is highly important.

4. Call to action

Surprisingly, this is where many miss it.

After you have developed their interests from the headline or subject and at the point where the order is to be made, you now have something like this:

"If you are willing to make an order, kindly click on the button."

You just told the prospect that they don't have to click on the button if they don't feel like it.

This is not the time to be nice. That's the time to give the command:

"Order Now"

In the days of newspaper ads, you could still afford to be nice. But this is the internet. The button leads to the payment page. In less than a minute, everything is over.

Ensure that your call-to-action button is clear. Let the color contrasts with the color of the background. It should appear as a button, not just as plain text.

- Your call to action does not have to be at the end of the page, let it be in the beginning, middle, and at the end.
- If you're offering a discount, let it also be on the button. Something like:

Order Today to Get 25% Off

Note:

You should remove ads, bells, and whistles on your landing page. The focus must be on the product you're selling. You don't want to distract the prospect with some blinking banner ads.

Some marketers ensure that only the call-to-action button is available on the landing page. Anyone who is not interested in the product can close the page altogether.

It does not give prospects an excuse to leave the page.

On Landing in Gmail's Primary Folder

Statistics from Gmail reveal that in 2020, about 1.8 billion people use the service. This makes it the dominant email service provider.

Chances are that most of your clients or subscribers receive your emails in their Gmail inboxes.

Only those who strictly run B2B services can say to an extent that their emails don't land in Gmail inboxes. Official inboxes receive most of those emails.

The Situation

The Gmail inbox is 100% behavioral. It aims to give the best user experience and it does this by categorizing emails into three main folders.

- The primary folder
- The social folder
- The promotions folder.

The primary folder gets what Gmail classifies as the most important and urgent.

The social folder gets what Gmail classifies as updates from social media accounts.

The promotions folder gets what Gmail classifies as promotional and marketing messages.

We are marketers and we *kinda* deserve to be in the promotions folder. However, we know from experience and statistics that most people only read their primary folder.

While I was a freelancer, I had access to some of my clients' business email accounts. Some of them would have hundreds of unread promotional emails.

We see emails in the primary folder as the really important ones. That's why an average marketer wants to get into the primary folder.

Tips on Getting into the Primary Folder

1. Use a blank or simple template

   Big brands use their custom-designed email templates and this makes sense. It gives them that corporate feel. However, they are flagged mostly as promotional emails.

It is much better to use a blank or simple template that is free of elements that scream corporate promotion. Let the email be as if you're sending it to a friend.

2. Avoid authority keywords

Keywords like Facebook, Google, Yahoo, Bing, Twitter, and YouTube are authority keywords. They echo promotions to Gmail and it flags them.

Instead of saying 'Google', you can say 'the biggest search engine in the world'. You can refer to Facebook as FB.

3. Write unique emails

In many affiliate programs, they offer email swipes. As much as this is helpful, many affiliates just copy the template, change a word or two, and send.

To the affiliate, the email template is tested and trusted and should bring in more sales. To Gmail, a lot of people are sending this, it must be promotional.

And how does Gmail know this? Just as it checks for uniqueness when it comes to SEO, it also checks for uniqueness in emails.

This is why you should write unique emails. Add your

voice to the email and let it sound personal.

You can use the email swipe. However, give it a personal touch. Don't just send what everyone else is sending.

4. Avoid stock photos as much as you can

I know, this is tough. However, the internet has gotten tired of the "perfection" in stock photos, they need something more realistic.

And Gmail knows this. It scrubs every photo.

You should use amateur photos. This can be a picture taken from your phone, screenshots, personal pictures, or any other photo that isn't stock.

If you have no other choice than to use stock photos, doctor them, edit them, and make them your own. You can do this with PowerPoint, Photoshop, Canva, or any other tool you find.

5. Symbol formats

Here, I mean the exclamations, boldface, and italics. These are good and needful. However, use them moderately.

When you use them a lot, they can trigger the promotions folder. The key is to make the email look as personal as possible.

6. Certain words

First, avoid curse words.

Second, as much as you use words like "last chance", 'free", "buy here", "click here", "guarantee", use them moderately. Overusing them can make you look aggressive. And aggressiveness can trigger either the promotions or the spam folder.

7. Personalize

When you're collecting contact details, get the first names. With personalization, there is a higher chance of landing in the primary folder. Use the first name in the subject line and, more importantly, use the first name at the beginning and the body of the copy.

Conclusion

The average prospect faces a lot of distractions. Both traditional and internet marketing are vying for attention. Big brands have the money to constantly bid on traffic, while small brands work hard to maximize every penny.

Always remember that the first step is grabbing attention. Once you have that attention, heighten curiosity, and boldly call the prospect to take action.

ABOUT THE AUTHOR

John is the Founder and Lead Content Creator of Woken Living. He is also the Lead Coach at the Content Development Masterclass.

John has been a professional content writer for about two years. Before setting out on his own, John worked as a content writer for a number of Digital Marketing companies. He has also worked with some startups in developing content strategies.

John teaches freelancing and how to write for the internet. Apart from writing professionally, he also writes as a pastime. He blogs and also writes short stories. He is a fan of The Lonely Island.

John is the Founder and Editor of Interesting African Stories - a Medium publication.